PROFESSIONAL PROSPERITY
FOR LAWYERS

PROFESSIONAL PROSPERITY FOR LAWYERS

FIND THE PERFECT JOB AND CREATE YOUR IDEAL CAREER

GREG YATES

PROFESSIONAL PROSPERITY PRESS

ORDERING INFORMATION:

Quantity sales. Special discounts are available on quantity pur-chases by corporations, associations, and others. For details, contact the publisher at the address above.

Orders by U.S. trade bookstores and wholesalers. Please con-tact Professional Prosperity Press: Tel: (212) 765-0685 or visit www.gregyatesconsulting.com.

Printed in the United States of America

TABLE OF CONTENTS

with little thought or vision of a career path. I subscribed to the time-tested "winging it" school of career planning.

In my last year of college, I applied to law school. I didn't even know a lawyer. I'd never talked to a lawyer. The decision to attend, or more accurately be enrolled in, law school was rather impulsive. I didn't understand the legal world or what it meant to work as a lawyer. That unexamined spontaneity was to become a hallmark of my career story.

I didn't like law school from the first day. I barely finished the first year. Then, I dropped out.

The federal government stepped in to rescue me. I received a generous stipend to get a Master's Degree in Public Administration. The government got no return on its investment in me. I had no interest in pursuing a civil service career.

With a little prodding from my family, I went back and finished law school. To relieve the boredom of the ordeal, I also completed an MBA. I found business much more interesting than the law. Business strategy and finance fascinated me.

Having proudly graduated in the top 75% of my law school class, I marched forward into my career. I was hired by a Fortune 100 company. My salary equaled the highest salary in my class; only the law review editor made as much. And, I didn't even have to take the bar exam. What luck!

Why did I have that luck? Because I didn't follow the traditional career path of a law school graduate into a law firm, a corporate legal department, or the government. I rejected it. Instead, I followed what I later called my "practical passion." Practical passion is an important concept which I will talk more about later. Practical passion is found where the activities you enjoy and the skills you excel at intersect with what other people want and will pay you to provide.

My career path was a crooked road. After a few years in the corporate world, I left to teach business in several universities and colleges, and worked with a few small businesses.

At that point, I took my first bar exam. Then I clerked for two federal judges. One in a small town in Alabama, the other in New York City.

I moved on and practiced law for the first time in my career at a well-known real estate boutique in New York. After several years, I moved to Florida to become in-house counsel for a publicly traded investment company. A few years later I moved again, this time to an Am Law 100 firm in Washington DC. After two years, I became an equity partner. A year later, I was asked to move back to New York City to open a new office for the firm. After a few years, I moved to my final legal position as an equity partner at another Am Law 100 firm.

During my legal career, I built a book of business of over $3.5 million a year. I represented several of the largest financial institutions in the world. And, I brought home a seven figure income for a number of years.

What the outside world didn't see in my career story was decades of boredom and stress. Dislike of and disengagement from my work. Substance abuse and bouts of depression. Divorce and financial issues. And, consideration of suicide on more than one occasion. I had never wanted to be a lawyer. I viewed myself as an impostor, and was alone in a crowd of colleagues and acquaintances. I could not enjoy the fruits of my career "success" story.

I learned more from my failures than from my successes. Some of my biggest professional successes contributed to some of my worst personal failures. I hope to share the lessons I learned in a way that allows you to avert similar experiences.

I am now on a mission. A mission to help you avoid having your career become a tragedy. Instead, I will help you create an epic career of success, prosperity, and personal fulfillment. Success, prosperity, and personal fulfillment as you, and only you, define them.

I will show you how to create your epic career story by using my career revitalization process. It's a simple process, but it takes action and hard work to implement. Fortunately, the rewards are well worth it.

HOW TO USE THIS BOOK

I discuss lawyer career revitalization in a broad way in order to allow every lawyer, from a law school student to an Am Law 100 senior equity partner, to use this book. Every lawyer will find insights and tips they can use now with their specific career issues to achieve success, prosperity, and personal fulfillment. The essential requirement is that you not only read this book, but that you use the information by taking action on it.

The book is organized in a modular format to make it easy for you to read and implement. You can use the complete career revitalization process, or apply specific sections to move you along your career path. The chapters are self-contained, independent, and include cross-references where necessary for context.

While you may read the chapters in any order, I recommend you read (or at least skim) the book from cover to cover. I suggest you at least read through to the end of the Management chapter before skipping around. That material will give you the philosophy and framework of the career revitalization process. It will also give you perspective as you read the other chapters.

You might want to start by reading a few of the transition scenarios in the Appendix. You'll get an idea of some of the typical scenarios for lawyers implementing the career revitalization process and also a brief glimpse into how the process works in practice.

There are questions and exercises throughout the book. I cannot urge you strongly enough to take the time to answer the questions and do the exercises. Answer the questions and do the exercises with pen and paper or on your computer, not just by thinking about the issues raised. To make it easier for you, I have compiled the questions and exercises in a workbook available in both PDF and Word format on my website (gregyates-consulting.com/professional-prosperity-for-lawyers). I suggest you head on over there now and print or download a copy to keep handy as you read.

You will increase the impact this book has on your professional career revitalization by at least ten times, if not a hundred times, if you take the time to answer the questions and complete the exercises. The process will help you find the perfect job, and create your ideal career. When you finish answering the questions and working through the exercises, you will have your personalized strategic career plan, goal list, and action plan. You will be prepared to take the exact steps necessary to achieve success, prosperity, and personal fulfillment.

I use a few conventions to help the flow of the narrative. **These words are used broadly and are inclusive of other terms, as noted:**

- "Employer" - An employer hires lawyers and pays them a salary for their services. This has usually been a firm, business, or the government. Clients also hire lawyers directly and pay them for their services. I use the word "employers" to include anyone who hires a lawyer, either directly or indirectly, to provide their services. The term "employer" applies to both traditional employer/employee relationships and to self-employment contexts. Often, a lawyer may have more than one employer, as they do when they work at a firm. Those lawyers' primary employers are their respective firms, and their secondary employers are their clients.

- "Job" - I use the word "job" to refer to work for pay, whether working for an employer or self-employed.

- "Services" - Lawyers provide services. Businesses provide services and products. I use the word "services" to include both services and products.

- When you have questions about what you read or how to apply it to your career, send me an email at gyates@gregyatesconsulting.com. You will receive a direct response from me.

First, you must view your career as a business. Whether you are a lawyer at the largest law firm in the world or a sole practitioner, you are a business. Your career should be run like a business.

Second, run your business as an entrepreneur if you want to be successful, prosperous, and personally fulfilled.

If you want to take charge of your future and realize your dreams of the perfect job and ideal career, the career revitalization process provides the framework. Use the framework, follow the process, and take the actions. You will find the perfect job and create your ideal career. A career giving you the freedom to do the work you want to do. When you want to do it. And, with the people you want to do it with.

Imagine getting up in the morning and looking forward to your day. Being rested and full of energy. Controlling your schedule. Working on projects that interest and excite you. Collaborating with people you like and respect. Taking time off to spend with family and friends. Having time for leisure activities or working on projects outside of your job.

The career revitalization process is grounded in the practices, processes, and actions of many lawyers who are successful, prosperous, and personally fulfilled. You can live your dreams by implementing the career revitalization process.

THE LEGAL INDUSTRY TODAY

The legal industry is in a period of transition. Disruption is in the air. Competition from other lawyers and non-lawyers is increasing. Unbundling, Alternative Legal Service Providers, AIternative Fee Arrangements, Contract Lawyers, Legal Tech, and New Law... terms rarely used ten years ago are now part of the legal industry lexicon.

Lawyers' roles are evolving at a fast pace. The demand for lawyers' services, as traditionally delivered, is decreasing. Lawyers are exiting and entering jobs much more frequently. Because of the disruptions in the legal industry, the role of a lawyer needs significant rewrites from the traditional legal career story.

Whether you call it Free Agent Nation, Freelancers United, Uberization, or the Gig Economy, the implications are the same. Lawyers and other professionals will not escape this global trend. The legal industry and lawyers are already experiencing the effects of the early stages of these trends. From the rising use of contract lawyers to the frequent moves of rainmakers.

The world is changing rapidly. Our profession is being transformed. Lawyers who thought they had a great job, and a clear career path in early 2008, quickly discovered their jobs could disappear in a heartbeat and, with them, their bright career paths. On average, lawyers change jobs every 4.2 years – sometimes voluntarily, other times not. Each time a lawyer changes jobs, the probability increases that their next job will be more like an independent contractor, as opposed to an employee.

Many lawyers see the current situation as a threat, and fight against the disruptive forces, attempting to defend an outdated system that no longer serves many of those it's meant to serve. A few lawyers see it as an exciting opportunity. I hope you are one of those.

LAWYER CAREER REVITALIZATION

Lawyers reconsider their career at certain points in their life. Before enrolling in law school, when they look for their first job after law school, and when employment opportunities arise. When they find they are so stressed or bored and realize something has to change. When they are fired or when their practice group leader makes a lateral move. Or, when there is a firm merger or bankruptcy.

A life change may also cause a lawyer to reconsider their career. Marriage or divorce. Health problems of their own or of a family member. Starting a family. Nearing retirement age, formal or informal. A growing desire to start their own business, either in the law or outside of it.

The cause of a lawyer's career reconsideration can be triggered by the desire to move toward a better career path or away from a failing career path. However, finding the perfect job and creating your ideal career is not done in isolation. Everything happening in your career and life must be considered before you engage in extensive work to find the perfect job and create your ideal career.

Lawyer career revitalization is not a one-and-done thing.

CAREER PLANNING

What was your first career plan? **Until recently, a typical lawyer's career plan was:**

1. Go to law school, get a job as an associate, and became an equity partner after seven or eight years of hard work.

2. 2. If you didn't like the work or the firm, you bailed out after a few years and went to another firm or in-house.

3. 3. Then, you worked for the next thirty years, advancing up the firm or corporate latter.

Simple as 1, 2, 3. Career plan, done. Next.

That method of career planning worked well for many lawyers for a long time. The legal industry was growing fast, opportunities were abundant, and compensation levels were hitting new records every year. You either followed the traditional career path or took one of the other opportunities available if not satisfied.

Then, the Big One. The Recession of 2008. Oh, sh__. A significant part of the legal industry suffered and many individual lawyers were decimated.

Many lawyers' career paths reached a dead end, or at least a dangerous curve in the road. Crisis mode took over, and lawyers' career focus became short-term. This shift was an economic necessity for many.

Now, seven years later, the legal industry has become a little more stable. But, the legal industry is different than it was in 2008. Corporate spending on traditional legal services provided by firms is still trending down. Lawyers at all levels face increasing competition from other lawyers and non-lawyers. The legal industry will never be the same. Lawyers' careers will never be the same. Your legal career plan will never be the same. It's time for you to go through a career revitalization process to find the perfect job and create your ideal career.

HOW TO CREATE A LAWYER CAREER REVITALIZATION PLAN

How can you have a fulfilling career and a happy life? By creating a career plan based on your interests and the skills you excel at, in line with your purpose and passions, and designed to lead to your vision of the perfect job and ideal career.

"Ugh that sounds like a lot of work, and I'm busy right now – maybe next year. Or the year after?"

The problem with procrastination and delay is that, without a plan, you will not dictate your career path. You may get lucky. You may not. A career plan will help you deal with the disruptive forces now prevalent in the legal industry. You also need a career plan in order to be prepared to seize fortuitous opportunities appearing in your path that may lead to the perfect job and ideal career.

Do you want to leave your career path up to forces you don't control? Wouldn't you feel more powerful if you took control and had a plan to find the perfect job and create your ideal career? I thought so.

Once you decide to take control of your legal career, the first question is usually: "Where do I start?"

The career revitalization planning process is comprised of two phases:

1. Assessing where you are now and envisioning your ideal career; and

2. Creating a strategic plan, goal list, action plan, and ac-

countability checks to find the perfect job and create your ideal career.

In the first phase of the career revitalization process, you evaluate where you are now in all areas of your career and life. You focus on rediscovering your purpose and passions. You envision your perfect career and life.

In evaluating yourself today, the focus is on your knowledge, skills, interests, and personality – particularly your strengths in these areas. You rediscover your purpose and find your passions. Doing work you are passionate about provides zest in your career and life, and lays the base for your success, prosperity, and personal fulfillment. Envisioning the perfect job and your ideal career with specificity gives you a target. A target that will inspire, energize, and motivate you.

In the second phase of the career revitalization process you formulate plans and set goals to take you from where you are today to the perfect job and ideal career. This phase comprises steps for acquiring knowledge about jobs you think may be a good fit for you. Steps for setting specific, measurable goals you can achieve within a set time. And, steps for taking action to move toward the perfect job and ideal career.

You research and identify jobs and career options where your purpose, passions, strengths, interests and vision converge. You set goals to achieve which will move you forward on your ideal career path. You create an action plan to specify the actions you will take to reach your goals and create your ideal career. Accountability is necessary at this stage of the career revitalization process.

YOUR FUTURE

As a lawyer, you have the opportunity to be an entrepreneurial business owner. Seize the reins now and take control of your future. You can create the career of your dreams by adopting the mindset and practices of an entrepreneur in a growing business.

Much of the stress and disengagement from your work results from not feeling any sense of control. By operating as an entrepreneurial businessperson, you'll feel more in control of your career and life. While, at least at first, you won't work any less, the sense of control you feel will reduce your stress and increase your engagement.

You can create a business, in or out of law, which will produce more financial rewards than many Big Law equity partners receive. You can have the flexibility to live your life the way you want to live it. If you want to travel, you can do so. And have time to spend with your kids and spouse. Time to enjoy life.

You don't have to leave the law to create this future. Remember, all the goodies come from viewing your career as a well-run business and having an entrepreneurial mindset.

You control your future. You have an ever-increasing set of tools to help you control your future. You also have opportunities never before available. Your future is unlimited if you adopt the mindset of an entrepreneurial businessperson. Yes, your world will differ from the world of lawyers in the past. And, it will be better.

Unless you desperately want to climb the Big Law Mountain, you can create your career path without being beholden to an extended apprenticeship system. A system where only a small percentage of associates ever become Big Law equity partners. And even if you are a mountain climber, this book will give you a process and the tools to make your climb easier and more enjoyable.

You can achieve success, prosperity and personal fulfillment by following the career revitalization process laid out in the rest of this book.

CHAPTER 2
THE FRAMEWORK

Lawyers' career issues are as different as each lawyer. Yet, career issues all point to finding the perfect job and creating your ideal career. That is what this book is about – how you can find the perfect job and create your ideal career. I wish I could work with every one of you on a personal level. Unfortunately, that is not possible.

The next best thing to working together is to present a framework and process for finding the perfect job and creating your ideal career. I'll introduce the framework of the career revitalization process before I talk about the individual parts of the process.

YOUR CAREER REVITALIZATION AS A BUSINESS TURNAROUND

I was a corporate turnaround, reorganization, and bankruptcy lawyer. My purpose as a lawyer was to help distressed companies successfully turn around and reorganize their businesses. I worked with owners, executives, and managers who were overworked, stressed, and miserable. A few were just bored, waiting for a pink slip. Most were frightened and had uncertain futures.

I now work with lawyers who don't have a clear path leading to their perfect job and ideal career. Many of them are going through experiences comparable to those of the owners, executives, and managers of distressed businesses.

In assisting lawyers without clear career paths, the similarities between those lawyers and the owners, executives, and managers of a distressed company became evident. I realized I could use my knowledge and experience from the corporate turnaround and restructuring world to assist lawyers without a clear career path. Lawyers with distressed careers.

The chart below shows various functions of distressed businesses that corporate turnaround professionals consider in their work. It also displays the corresponding areas of lawyers' careers and the underlying ideas of the career revitalization process:

DISTRESSED BUSINESS	LAWYERS CAREER	IDEA
Management	Purpose & Vision	Reconsider & Re-Vision
Inventory	Skills & Interests	Resources
Research & Development	Services	Research
Strategic Planning & Implementation	Strategic Plan, Goal List & Action Plan	Revitalize
Marketing & Sales	Personal Branding & Promotion	Relationships
Information Technology	Tools & Reflection	Review

If you view your career as a distressed business, what can you learn from successful corporate turnaround professionals? Three overarching concepts stand out:

URGENCY & FOCUS

Corporate turnaround professionals work with a sense of urgency and focus. When retained, these professionals are on the ground immediately and on high alert. A potentially successful business turnaround may become liquidation because of a few days' delay in taking action.

Once you start to revitalize your career, either in or out of the law, act with urgency and focus on the things that make a significant impact. Do this whether you are facing a current career crisis or not. You never know when what you think are minor issues will explode all over your career. You must be proactive.

ACCURATE DATA

Corporate turnaround professionals must have reliable data about the business in order to know where to focus. Their examination of the current state of the company relies on hard data and subjective judgments. The professionals complete their first analysis quickly to provide a base for immediate decisions and actions. Comprehensive, detailed analysis of major problem areas is a continuing process.

As a lawyer with a distressed career, you need accurate data. You need to honestly assess where you are now in your career and life. You need to be clear on your purpose and passions. You need to know your strengths. You need a detailed vision of the perfect job and ideal career. Once you have this information, you can begin to revitalize your distressed career.

MASSIVE ACTION

Corporate turnaround professionals make decisions quickly and then take action. If a business is distressed, whatever the cause, it must be addressed immediately. The mission and goals of a distressed business may not change, but there must be a radical shift in some areas of the company for a successful turnaround. Massive focused action is crucial for a successful revitalization of the company.

To revitalize your career, you must take massive action. However, focused action based on accurate data is required.

We'll look at how corporate turnaround professionals approach a distressed business. We'll then apply lessons from the corporate turnaround world to the process of successfully revitalizing your career.

YOU ARE A BUSINESS

Did you realize you were going into business for yourself when you started law school? That you would be a business owner? Have you realized it yet? Welcome to your career as a lawyer – YOU, LLP, Attorney at Law.

It doesn't matter if you're a Big Law attorney or a solo practitioner. It doesn't matter if you work at a firm, as in-house counsel, or are using your legal education in some other way. It doesn't matter if you are an associate, a partner, or unemployed. You own a business: YOU, LLP, Attorney at Law.

You went to law school to work as a lawyer in a firm, business, or the government. To someday advance to partner or general counsel. You might still be on that path. But, you consider yourself as an employee unless you're a solo practitioner, an equity partner in a small firm, or a top rainmaker in Big Law.

If you keep the employee mindset, whether you are an employee or an owner (equity partner), you will severely limit your career opportunities. And, your chance for success, prosperity, and personal fulfillment. A lawyer with an employee mindset looks to an employer as being responsible for their career. You get hired by a firm, organization, or the government. Your belief is: "give me the ground rules for what I need to do, and I'll do it well and then be promoted to the next level." Kind of like the way your academic career evolved.

The employee mindset is becoming less and less viable as a mindset for a successful career – not just in law, but in any profession. It worked well for many lawyers until 2008. For at least 30 years before 2008, the legal industry was a fast-growing industry providing plentiful opportunities for lawyers and ever-increasing financial rewards. No longer.

Today, the legal industry is continuing to go through uncertain times with little growth, disruption of traditional business models, and increased competition. Law firms dissolve or merge regularly. Fewer and fewer firm lawyers are advancing to being equity partners. There is little growth in the number of law firm jobs. Corporate law departments are using more non-lawyers and contract lawyers. There is increasing outsourcing of legal work, both domestically and to foreign lawyers and other providers.

The days of loyalty between employees and employers are long gone. So are the days of loyalty among partners of law firms. Partners and associates regularly leave their firms for what they believe to be better opportunities. And, even partners are let go by their firms if they don't produce business.

WHAT'S A LAWYER TO DO?

Lawyers creating successful, prosperous, and personally fulfilling careers think of themselves as businesses, not employees. This is true whether they practice in firms, businesses, government, or even if they leave the law for another career. While lawyers may continue to practice law, they can no longer consider themselves as working in the legal "profession." Today, they work in the legal industry.

When you view your career as a business, you need to know the best practices of successful businesses, and apply them to yourself and your career. The three most important business functions to focus on in your business are: management, strategic planning, and marketing.

A few of you may read the preceding paragraph, and after reflecting on it for a few minutes, say, "Yes, but isn't that what most successful lawyers are already doing?" You are correct. Many of the most successful lawyers – the rainmakers – instinctively know that managing their career as a business is the way to success.

Think about the lawyers you know or know about. Group the great technical lawyers. Group the most successful lawyers, usually the rainmakers. Do these two groups correspond to each other? In my experience, there is a significant area where the groups don't overlap.

Excellent technical lawyers are not always successful, and very successful lawyers are not always great technical lawyers. I equate success with monetary compensation for the purpose of this discussion. While compensation is not the measure of success for some lawyers, it is for many lawyers. Success is a personal concept for each attorney. Some great technical lawyers can be extremely successful lawyers within their own idea of success. But if those lawyers believe their technical skills will be rewarded with top compensation levels, they are mistaken.

You have now decided to manage your career as a business. Wonderful, best of luck! But, Yates, "now what?"

Go get an MBA. No, no, no, just kidding. Apply the concepts used in the business world to your job and career.

Okay, so now you have a map.

Why does someone start a business? Because they have a strong purpose and passion, sometimes referred to as their "Why." In business schools, the "why" is called a mission statement. Most companies have them. Mission statements include a business's purpose for providing the services it offers, and their vision for the future.

What is your purpose in your career and life? What is your "Why"? What is your vision of the future? Your answers are a rough draft of the mission statement of YOU, LLP, Attorney at Law.

How does a business determine what assets it has to operate and produce the services it offers? Right, it takes an inventory.

Take an inventory of yourself. In what area is your deepest knowledge? What are your top skills? Which aspects of your personality are the strongest? You are trying to identify your strengths, those things about you that are valuable in creating your ideal career. Those assets are what you will use to make

YOU, LLP, Attorney at Law into a business reflecting your mission statement.

HOW IS SUCCESS DEFINED FOR A BUSINESS? HOW DOES A COMPANY KNOW WHERE IT IS GOING?

The previous two questions are answered by a company's owners and executives. The answer is found in the owners' and executives' vision of the future. Their vision provides a target to define success. For most companies, profitability is the top measure of success. But even for those businesses, there are other measures that are also targets for the businesses' success.

How do businesses hit their targets and become successful? They create a strategic plan to serve as a guide for their vision of the business. The strategic plan is a roadmap for the company, to take them from where they are now to where they envision their future. Strategic plans help businesses reach their targets.

Lawyers operating as a business need a strategic plan to realize their vision. YOU, LLP, Attorney at Law requires a strategic plan and a list of goals for the future. These objectives are based on your vision of the future. The strategic plan and goal list will be your game plan for the future of your business.

WHAT GUIDES A BUSINESS'S DAY-TO-DAY OPERATIONS?

Companies use operating plans for the primary functions of their business. The operating plans detail how their business's goals will be realized. Operating plans specify the actions necessary to reach the company's goals.

What guides lawyers in managing their careers as businesses, and moving forward on their career paths to reach their goals? The same thing that guides a business. But, instead of referring to it as an operating plan, we call it an action plan.

ENTREPRENEURIAL MINDSET

It is not how your job is classified that is important; it is your mindset. You may be an employee with a great job, but until you adopt an entrepreneurial mindset, you will not realize your ideal career. Just as importantly, you will not be prepared to deal with unexpected events affecting your career. Adopting an entrepreneurial mindset will position you as a lawyer poised to conquer all obstacles in the way of your ideal career.

Associates, in-house counsel, and government lawyers must develop an entrepreneur's mindset if they want a successful career. Lawyers who take charge of their careers and act as entrepreneurs are more successful than other lawyers. They earn more money and are more satisfied with their careers and lives.

Many equity partners who own part of a business, their firm, do not consider themselves as business owners or entrepreneurs, but instead have an employee mindset. While these partners are owners, they act like employees and should expect the same consequences that employees find when a disruptive event affects their firm or practice group. It is time for these equity partners to adopt an entrepreneurial mindset. They need to consider themselves as entrepreneurial business owners of their career, even if they do not feel that way about their firm.

How does an entrepreneur act? These characteristics show an entrepreneurial mindset:

CONSISTENT ACTION

Entrepreneurs take action. Relentless action. Consistent action.

You don't find the perfect job or create your ideal career by taking frenetic action for a week and then doing nothing for the next month. It takes consistent, systematic action, if only for 15 minutes a day. The tortoise beats the hare every time.

If you invest just fifteen minutes a day on action directed toward creating your ideal career, during a year, you will devote over ninety hours to those actions. Spending thirty minutes a day is the same as working full-time for well over a month on creating your ideal career.

Lawyers with an entrepreneurial mindset take consistent action to create their ideal career. You find the perfect job and create your ideal career through the actions you take, not because of the ideas or plans you have. You've dreamed of the perfect job and ideal career often. But, most of us have fallen short of creating ideal careers. Far short.

From the time I was a teenager, I devoured self-help, career, and business books. I loved to learn new things and to be exposed to new ideas. I would get excited, thinking about how I could apply the wisdom in the books to my career and life. Over the years, I've collected hundreds and hundreds of those books. Bookcases full of them line most walls in my apartment. I even pay for storage space for boxes filled with books. The Kindle has fed my addiction.

Did these books help me create an ideal career? No! Why? Because I didn't take action to implement what I read. While the knowledge was valuable, it was almost worthless until I put it into action. To have created an ideal career path to success, prosperity, and personal fulfillment, I would have had to apply the ideas in those books. However, after finishing a book, I seldom took action to implement the ideas. Instead, I picked up the next book in the stack. Taking consistent action to implement ideas was a missing ingredient in creating my vision of an ideal career.

PASSION

One of the most important characteristics of lawyers with an entrepreneurial mindset is passion. Their passion might be civil rights, hostile takeovers, or trial advocacy. The nature of their passion is not important. The passion itself is what fuels the success of these lawyers.

We all know passionate lawyers. They love their work. They talk about their work constantly, and are happy and engaged with their work and career.

Self-motivation results from their passions. Passionate lawyers jump out of bed in the morning, ready to take on new challenges. They have more energy, focus, and enthusiasm for their work than other lawyers.

Passion fuels action, but to what end? Lawyers with entrepreneurial mindsets also possess a vision.

VISION

Having a vision of the future is another important characteristic of a lawyer with an entrepreneurial mindset. A vision based on their passions. These lawyers think about the big picture. Not only the next client, deal, or case.

Vision is a long-term concept. Entrepreneurial lawyers envision the future in detail. Their vision guides everything they do. Every goal they set and every action they take is focused on moving them closer to their vision of an ideal career.

Some lawyers have a vision, but they don't seem able to move toward that vision. Why? Because they are not tenacious.

TENACITY

Tenacity is another important characteristic of the entrepreneurial mindset. Tenacity means "keeping a firm hold". Tenacious lawyers seldom give up or become discouraged. They keep a firm hold on their vision of the future.

Being tenacious does not mean you are aggressive, overbearing, or obnoxious. Instead, it means you are perseverant and resilient.

Tenacity is built on, but separate from, passion. It is hard to be tenacious without having passion, but some lawyers with passion lack tenacity. To be a successful lawyer or a success in any other occupation requires a positive "can do" attitude. Besides the attitude, consistent action must follow.

A lawyer's tenacity is tested in the face of adversity, disappointments, and setbacks. The ability to continue working toward their vision of the future, despite tough circumstances, is the mark of an entrepreneurial lawyer.

Why are some lawyers tenacious while others are not? Self-belief.

SELF-BELIEF

Lawyers with an entrepreneurial mindset believe in themselves. This characteristic is more than self-confidence. It is self-confidence with an underlying belief in their vision.

Self-belief is not based on an inflated ego and is not arrogant. A lawyer with self-belief may be reserved and relaxed.

Entrepreneurial lawyers who believe in themselves don't believe they are self-sufficient. Instead, they know their strengths and limitations, and they work with others to express their passions and realize their vision.

TOLERATION OF AMBIGUITY

An occupational hazard of being a lawyer is having difficulty tolerating ambiguity. Much of our work is undertaken to clarify ambiguity and to minimize risk. This mindset is baked into us from the first day of law school.

The inability to tolerate ambiguity or to take reasonable risks is one of the major reasons some lawyers never achieve career success. Lawyers with an entrepreneurial mindset can tolerate ambiguity and take measured risks. Entrepreneurial lawyers tolerate ambiguity and take measured risks because of their passion and self-belief.

FLEXIBILITY

Lawyers with an entrepreneurial mindset are flexible. They are ready to react to situations as they occur, based on whatever seems most appropriate at the time.

Entrepreneurial lawyers are not constrained by the way things have always been done. They are not bound by traditional ideas about the law or how to practice. These lawyers are more attuned to finding solutions that fit a specific situation.

Flexible lawyers are imaginative. They consider ideas outside of standard practice and tradition. Lawyers with flexibility and vision look to other practice areas or disciplines outside of the law in order to find solutions to issues. One way in which entrepreneurial lawyers spark creativity is taking ideas from different areas and applying them in new contexts.

The cornerstones of an entrepreneurial lawyer are action, passion, vision, tenacity, self-belief, toleration of ambiguity, and flexibility. The more of these traits you incorporate into your mindset, the quicker your career revitalization will result in the perfect job and ideal career.

CONCEPTS

The career revitalization process is based on four concepts.

First, finding the perfect job and creating your ideal career is a holistic endeavor. When you envision the perfect job and ideal career, you consider all areas of your life, not just your career.

Second, your idea of the perfect job and vision of an ideal career will be informed by your strengths and interests. You may have visions (possibly hallucinogenic) of being a Supreme Court Justice. But, if your strength or interest is not in the detailed intellectual analysis of arcane constitutional issues, reconsider your vision of being addressed as Justice Big Shot.

Third, collaboration with others is essential. Seeking and accepting help throughout the career revitalization process is crucial. Whether the help is from family, friends, colleagues, mentors, advisers, consultants, or coaches, working collaboratively with them will be invaluable in your career revitalization process.

Fourth, you will need to apply certain economic and business concepts while working through and implementing the career revitalization process. Don't worry – I won't go all mathematical on you like an Econ professor. You will just use concepts that are more common sense than anything.

SUCCESS, PROSPERITY AND PERSONAL FULFILLMENT IS HOLISTIC

Success, prosperity, and personal fulfillment in your career is directly related to fulfilling your purpose in life. You may have a purpose or multiple purposes in each area of your career and life. In your career, you may strive for professional recognition and high income. In your personal life, you may want close relationships and the freedom to pursue non-work-related activities.

Success, prosperity, and personal fulfillment are reflected in your ability to achieve your goals not only in your career, but in the rest of your life. The holy grail of the work-life balance. We all know lawyers who appear very successful in their careers by any measure of success, but whose personal lives are a mess. These lawyers have not prioritized and focused on areas of their lives outside of their careers.

In planning your ideal career path, you need to consider all areas of your life, not just your career. Your focus, time, and effort may be concentrated on your job for certain periods of time in the career revitalization process. But, if this continues for too long, success, prosperity, and personal fulfillment in your life will be derailed.

What areas of your life are most important for you to consider in working through the career revitalization process? Besides areas relating to your career, look at your relationships with family, friends, and members of your community. Examine your physical, emotional, and spiritual life. Your physical life comprises your nutrition, fitness, and sleep. Your emotional life relates to how you manage stress, anxiety, boredom, or other troublesome emotions. Your spiritual life – and this is not synonymous with religious life – comprises your values, beliefs, and purpose in life.

UTILIZE YOUR STRENGTHS

You have skills you excel at and enjoy using. Those are the skills you will use in the perfect job and ideal career.

Both your strengths and interests must align if you are going to be successful, prosperous, and personally fulfilled. You may have skills you excel at, but you hate using. These are not skills you want to build your career around. One of the most prevalent and saddest of all career failures is the lawyer who has skills they excel at, and who develops a successful career around them, but hates what they are doing. Although outwardly successful, they are dying inside. If you don't like using specific skills or participating in certain activities, even if you are great at them, don't build your career around those skills or activities.

You may have a keen interest in an area, but weak skills. In some ways, this is the easier situation to deal with. It is easier to develop skills when interested in something than it is to develop an interest when you have skills. In other ways, it is harder to deal with. Even if you have great interest, you may not be able to develop the necessary skills. It may make sense, particularly early in your career, to attempt to develop skills required for areas that interest you. But, be careful to cut your losses if it becomes apparent that you will never have the skills to excel in that area.

Whatever your strengths and interests, build on them. Create new and innovative ways to use them. Continue to refine them.

While traditional career management advice is to develop your skills in areas where you are weak, that is a loser's game. The reason you may be weak in a particular area is that you aren't interested in it. Because you didn't have an interest in an area, you never spent the time to develop your skills. Know your weakness. But, instead of spending time and effort to develop your skills in areas where you are weak, look for ways to compensate by using other people to fill the gaps.

If you are a superstar in writing appellate briefs, but weak in oral argument, traditional career advice would be to work on your oral advocacy skills. Wrong. Your value is in your strengths. Use them. Build on them. You can collaborate with a colleague or hire someone with strong oral advocacy skills to do the oral arguments in your cases.

What about the lawyer who has not yet developed skills they excel at? The advice still holds, with slight refinement. If you are still developing skills you excel at, focus your efforts on those skills you gravitate toward and enjoy. You need enough exposure to an area to know what it is about and the skills needed to excel. But, work on building your strengths in areas where you are instinctively drawn and have an interest.

Successful, prosperous and personally fulfilled lawyers build their careers on their strengths. You can't be great at everything. Show the world your greatness and lead with your strengths.

COLLABORATION

I always tried to do everything myself. Part of this attitude I attribute to the fact that I seldom had a sense that others had my best interests at heart. Part of this belief sprung from my concept of self-reliance and individualism as being critical factors in growth and success in life. And, part of this attitude I ascribe to my deep-seated shame and the fear of being truthful and vulnerable with others. The impostor syndrome.

Networks

It took me many years to realize I needed the help of others, from family and friends to paid professionals. This realization that collaboration was a powerful force was critical for me in developing a life of success, prosperity, and personal fulfillment.

Your networks of personal and professional contacts can provide information, assistance, advice, and access to other people and resources. You must take consistent action to establish, maintain, and nurture your personal and professional networks. The contacts in your networks are excellent resources to use in meeting and connecting with other people who are in a position to help you advance along the path to your ideal career.

The most important thing to remember about any network is that the relationships must be mutual. You must assist others and give value to them before you can expect that they will help you. That is why a consistent focus on maintaining and nurturing contacts in your networks is essential.

Mentors

Using a mentor is an effective way to get honest advice on the perfect job and ideal career. Finding a mentor in the legal industry can be tough. Partners are busy and, in Big Law, the pyramid means that the vast majority of associates leave before they become partners. Partners seldom want to mentor lawyers who will leave within a few years.

Your best opportunity to find a mentor is to do great work for a partner and help make their life easier. The more valuable you are to them, the more likely you will be to establish a mentoring relationship.

Another good way to find a mentor is through bar (no, not bartenders) or professional organizations. Participate in professional and trade associations as part of your personal branding and networking activities. Look for someone senior to you who is doing work that would appear to be on your ideal career path, and who seems approachable. Try to build a relationship with them over time and they may agree to mentor you.

Mastermind Groups

Participating in a formal or informal mastermind group is a great way to collaborate with others to find the perfect job and create your ideal career. Mastermind groups are usually composed of anywhere from three to twelve. Between four and six or seven people is the best size for a mastermind group.

Mastermind groups for lawyers are composed of individuals around the same level, but usually from different firms, and a good one should include non-lawyer professionals. The idea is to have a group of smart people at around the same level in their careers who can brainstorm, give advice, cross-pollinate, and serve as cheerleaders and accountability partners. The mastermind group will not be effective unless there are strict attendance rules and total buy-in to the group by all members.

You can form a mastermind group yourself. Be thoughtful and intentional about who you ask to join. Try to find a good mix of people with different skills and perspectives, but enough shared interests to add cohesion to the group. You can meet over the phone or in person. The group should meet no less than once a month. A good rule is that, if someone misses more than one meeting, they are out. These groups can be valuable in helping you as you work through your career revitalization process. If you join someone else's group, or even if you start your own, know that many groups pay a monthly fee to the organizer for setting up the group.

Professionals

Other potential collaborators are consultants, advisers, and coaches. Although you are hiring these individuals to provide a service, the relationship almost always works best when based on collaboration between equals, not a teacher-student relationship. While there may be teaching and expert advice given, if it is a one-way conversation, you will not be happy with the relationship.

You can engage a broad range of consultants, advisers, and coaches to help you in different aspects of your career revitalization process. Be selective. These experts can be worth their weight in gold or worthless. I've engaged both types. Formal training and experience have little correlation to results. Effectiveness depends on the personal relationship established, and on the willingness and ability of the consultant, adviser, or coach to listen. The key is to find someone who will not just roll out the stock answers and solutions, but who will consider your unique situation and help you reach your specific goals.

ECONOMIC AND BUSINESS PRINCIPLES

Several economic and business principles are useful in working through and implementing your career revitalization process. These principles help you decide how to allocate your time, effort, and money to find the perfect job and create your ideal career. The principles give you alternative frameworks and perspectives for considering where to invest your time, effort, and money for maximum impact.

Opportunity Costs

The concept of opportunity costs, as it applies to lawyer career revitalizations, holds that when you spend your time in a certain activity, you are foregoing all the other activities you could do. If you spend an hour watching television, your opportunity cost of that time is the research, networking, or self-promotion activities you could have accomplished instead. In the big picture, what has more value? I suspect your answer is not watching Modern Family.

Using the principle of opportunity costs to allocate your time and energy allows you to focus on value. You can appreciate that, when you spend time on low-value activities, the opportunity cost of the higher value activities you didn't engage in is substantial. The moral is to spend your time on high-value activities in order to minimize your opportunity costs.

Law Of Diminishing Returns

The law of diminishing returns builds on marginal analysis. Marginal analysis looks at the result of adding one more unit of something and measuring the effect it has on a related item. If you eat one ice cream cone, how much satisfaction do you get? If you eat a second ice cream cone, do you get the same satisfaction, or more, or less? I suspect most of you would answer less. That is the law of diminishing returns in action. How does this relate to lawyer career revitalization?

In deciding what actions you take and what activities you engage in, continuing to do more of the same thing is not always the best use of your time. Even if it was very effective to begin with. If you start a research project on a particular employer, you will learn a lot of new information in your first hour of work. You will not learn as much in the second hour. Even less in the third hour. What you learn in the second and third hours, while not as much, may be important. The goal of applying the law of diminishing returns is to realize that your efforts will become less effective and efficient at some point. The key is to recognize when the value of your effort has decreased to a level where your time is better spent doing something else.

Return On Investment

Return on investment (ROI) is the value you get from the expenditure of your time or money. It's a core business concept, and one of the primary gauges of success for any investment. When you invest an hour of your time networking at a cocktail reception, what is your return? While the return on time at a cocktail party may be impossible to gauge in monetary terms, you have a general sense of the return.

The benefit of ROI analysis is in using it to compare different possible uses of your time or money. Is your hour better spent at a cocktail reception, making calls to old colleagues, or writing a blog post? The first question to answer is the measure of return you are focusing on. Is your return measured by having a good time at a social event or finding the perfect job? If the former is the case, clearly the cocktail party is how to go. If you are focused on finding the perfect job, perhaps making the calls or writing the blog post has more value.

In looking at the value of different activities, you will also confront a timing issue. The calls might produce more immediate value, but the blog post might be more valuable over the long-term, especially if you are planning to incorporate it into a book. For most of what you will do in the career revitalization process, measures of monetary returns will not be available. It will be your judgment on the value of a particular investment of time or money. It is beneficial to use the concept of ROI as a guide when thinking about how to spend your time and money in finding the perfect job and creating your ideal career.

Sunk Costs And Future Value

One of the most devious issues many lawyers face in making career transitions is the value they put on their past decisions, experiences, and expenditures. Many unhappy and disengaged lawyers say they could never consider changing career paths to leave the law, or even to look at another platform or way to practice. They believe they have invested far too much money and incurred too much debt in getting their law degree to turn in a different direction. These lawyers have spent years learning their craft and can't just "throw it away" to consider other jobs or career paths. Well, this line of thinking and analysis doesn't stand up under scrutiny. You may have heard the phrase, "Throwing good money after bad." That's where this line of thought leads. Economists refer to this as the sunk cost fallacy.

The theory of sunk costs holds that your prior investment decisions, whether of money or time, are not relevant to how you decide about your current investments of time or money. The only relevant factor is the future return you will get on the current investment, the ROI. If you're striving for success, prosperity, and personal fulfillment, will spending another year doing what you are doing be more valuable to you than using some of your time to find the perfect job and create your ideal career? Possibly, but it depends on your definition of future value.

The first measure of value that many lawyers consider is money. They believe that, if they transition from their current job to another job, they will not earn as much money, so any talk of career change is foolhardy. This may be true in the short-run, but not necessarily in the long-run. Yes, a career transition, particularly out of Big Law, may lead to an immediate reduction in income. But, if you project five years into the future, the income you will earn at that time may be greater if you transition your career path now instead of waiting for your current career to flame out.

However, as many lawyers, including me, have learned the hard way, money is not the be-all and end-all. Money doesn't buy happiness. Personal fulfillment is achieved by following your purpose and passions, using your strengths, and realizing that your ideal career may not be the one where you are earning the highest income.

The moral is that any consideration of your past investments of money or time, in regard to deciding your current and future investments, will lead to faulty decisions. The only thing that matters is the future return, measured in both monetary and non-monetary terms, on your current investment of money or time.

Important/Urgent

You can classify all the possible activities you could engage in as either important or unimportant, and either urgent or not urgent. This can be diagrammed in a four-box table.

1: Urgent And Important	2: Urgent And Not Important
3: Not Urgent And Important	4: Not Urgent And Not Important

Your goal is to spend most of your time doing important tasks. Unfortunately, the pull of everyday life and the natural inclination of many lawyers is to do the urgent tasks first. The unfortunate thing is that many of the important tasks are not urgent, and many of the unimportant tasks are urgent. If you do unimportant, but urgent tasks, the cost is leaving important but not urgent tasks undone. This is not a formula for success, prosperity, and personal fulfillment.

The urgency of our lives is compounded by constant email, phone calls, social media, and drop-by visitors. Each of these wants immediate attention. To focus on the important tasks, many of which are not urgent, you need to resist the false urgency inherent in your day. Only check your email at a few designated times each day. Don't answer your phone during intense, focused work periods. Turn off social media notifications, close your door, and put a "Do Not Disturb" sign on the outside of the door.

Only by concentrating on the important but not urgent tasks will you be able to focus on the career revitalization process. If you don't concentrate on the important activities, you will never find the perfect job, create your ideal career, and find success, prosperity, and personal fulfillment.

80/20 Rule (Pareto Principle)

The 80/20 Rule was first postulated by the Italian economist Vilfredo Pareto. The concept, as applied to your career revitalization process, holds that 80% of the results you achieve will come from 20% of the time you spend. It's the same concept as saying 80% of your firm's profits come from 20% of its clients.

The key to applying the 80/20 Rule is to identify which of your activities constitute the 20% that are most valuable, and which make up the 80% that are not nearly as valuable. Use your experience and judgment to apply the Rule to your situation. Be curious and attentive going forward to see if you can better judge the 20% of activities you should concentrate on to achieve 80% of the results.

Continual Learning

Little must be said about this principle. In today's world, unless you are continually learning new skills and soaking up new knowledge, others will pass you by. Your effectiveness and efficiency will drop off if you are not staying up to date, and your productivity will take a dive.

Be intentional about what you want to learn and how you gain the knowledge. Learning about the latest Hollywood gossip or the news of the day is not knowledge – only information. Look for great blogs, articles, and books to read. Take a live or online course to strengthen skills you excel at. Keep exercising your mental muscles to stay strong and ready to compete to find the perfect job and create your ideal career.

CHAPTER 3

MANAGEMENT (PURPOSE, PASSIONS & VISION)

MANAGEMENT IN DISTRESSED BUSINESSES

It's the people who are most important in a business. The ownership and management of a business are crucial to its success. A corporate turnaround professional's initial evaluation of ownership and management focuses on two areas. What are the individual's purposes and passions, and what are their visions for the future of the business?

Turnaround professionals confirm that the owners and management of a business share the same purpose, passions, and vision. One cause of a distressed business is when owners and individual members of management have different and varying purposes, passions, and visions. These differences must be resolved in order to create unity for a successful revitalization of the company.

If there's not a shared purpose, passion, and vision, the focus, resolve, and enthusiasm to accomplish the turnaround will be lacking. Chances of success will be less than average. The turnaround professionals work with the owners and management to devise a shared purpose, passion, and vision for a successful turnaround of the business.

MANAGEMENT IN YOUR DISTRESSED CAREER REVITALIZATION

Management issues in distressed businesses correspond to the issues of purpose, passion, and vision for lawyers with distressed careers.

Think of your career as a distressed business. You are the owner and manager of YOU, LLC, Attorney at Law. **Ask yourself these two questions:**

- What are your purpose and passions?
- What is your vision of the perfect job and ideal career?

Take the time to reflect on the questions and answer them in writing. You will begin to understand the causes of your distressed career. A glimmer of light on the path to your distressed career revitalization may also appear.

Review your past to help clarify your purpose and passions. Determine what is important to you and identify your purpose in life. This step is crucial for successful career revitalization. Consideration of your deepest values and beliefs may help you to isolate your purpose and passions. Focus on your purpose and passions in finding the perfect job and creating your ideal career. This will lead you to success, prosperity, and personal fulfillment – not only in your career, but in your life.

After rediscovering your purpose and passions, you then need to envision the perfect job and ideal career at various times, and with great specificity. Until you know where you want to go, how will you create an action plan to get you there? To revitalize your career, take the advice of Stephen Covey to "begin with the end in mind." Once you flesh out your vision, work on your career revitalization can proceed.

REDISCOVERING YOUR PURPOSE & PASSIONS

Review and reconsider your past. It is the best way to find your purpose and passions. In reviewing your past, you will rediscover you core beliefs, values, and purpose in life. You will also rediscover your passions.

Your ideal career is founded on your purpose and passions. Many lawyers who are disengaged from their work and unhappy in their careers have lost the connection between the work they do and their purpose and passions. A primary aim of the career revitalization process is reconnecting you with your purpose and passions, and helping you to align your work and career with your purpose and passions.

The questions and exercises in the following sections guide you through doing the archaeological work on your past. You will rediscover the parts of yourself that make you who you are and prepare you for success, prosperity, and personal fulfillment. There are exercises designed to help you uncover your purpose and passions. This will help you build a solid foundation for your ideal career. Please do the exercises. Not just in your head, but in writing. The effectiveness of your work is magnified many times over by writing your responses to the exercises.

PURPOSE AND PASSION

You're a lawyer. You may be early in your career. Or, you might have been practicing for a long time.

Unfortunately, you don't like your current job. The long hours and stress are killing you. Your work is not engaging, and you are bored. You are not making an impact in the world. You don't make enough money. People you work with are jerks.

Whatever your particular reasons, you've reached the point where you are reconsidering your job and career path.

Wonderful! But, where do you start?

By looking at your past. Specifically, by looking at your past to rediscover your purpose and passions.

These questions and exercises will help you reconsider your past and rediscover your purpose and passions. You will find these questions and exercises, and all other questions and exercises in this book, including additional material not found in the book, in a complementary workbook on my website (greg-yatesconsulting.com/professional-prosperity-for-lawyers). It is available for download in both PDF and Word format.

LIFE HISTORY EXERCISE

What did you want to be when you grew up? A doctor, lawyer, or Indian chief? A rock star, firefighter, or professional athlete?

Remember what you wanted to be when you were younger. It will give you insight into your ideal career path. Nope, this doesn't mean you should quit your job and pursue a career as a rock star or professional athlete. The real benefit of considering what you wanted to be when you grew up is to identify your purpose in life, your "Why". Don't focus on the "what" you wanted to do when you grew up, but instead focus on "why" you wanted to do it.

For some lawyers, the answer is that they wanted to be a lawyer when they grew up. Why? Because they saw television shows or movies about lawyers and thought lawyers' lives looked fun and exciting. Unfortunately, now you are a lawyer and you know the television and movie versions of lawyers are not reality. Far from it.

Other lawyers wanted to be lawyers when they grew up because their family decided that was the right career for them. Again, this rarely works well since you followed someone else's dream, not your own.

Even lawyers who always knew they wanted to be lawyers also had periods where they wanted to be something else. If you didn't always want to be a lawyer, maybe you wanted to be a teacher, an astronaut, or a policeman. Why? You wanted to help other people. You wanted excitement and adventure. You wanted to wear a uniform.

Did you want to be an archaeologist or an astronomer? Why? You liked to learn and explore new ideas. You wanted to experiment and discover new things.

Go back to your younger days and remember what you wanted to be when you grew up. You wanted to be different things at different times. Remember them all. Now, think back and identify the reasons you dreamed about those occupations. What were you passionate about? What motivated you?

Was your purpose fame, fortune, adventure, freedom, knowledge, discovery, power, or a desire to help others? Or, something else? The key is to remember what turned you on, what you were passionate about, and what motivated you.

How did what you want to be change over time? Did you have a clear idea from an early age which you stayed focused on? Or, did you change your idea of your dream career as you got older, and gained more knowledge about yourself and particular occupations? Continue searching for why you changed.

Stop this inquiry into your past when you reach the point where your "why" became "it was practical." While practicality is worth considering in creating your ideal career path, it's not relevant at this stage of the career revitalization process. We all must have food and shelter. But it's your purpose and passions that lead to a career path where you are energized and motivated. Where you will find success, prosperity, and personal fulfillment.

The whole point of considering what you wanted to be when you grew up is to identify your purpose and passions. The things you got jazzed about. Things that interested and excited you.

Do thoughts about what you wanted to do when you were younger still excite you? Do you think, "what if"?

Is so, you have a starting place for building a foundation to revitalize your career path. Your perfect job and ideal career will incorporate your purpose and passions. Energy and motivation will be the result. Without those elements, your job is just a way to earn a living – with the stress, drudgery, and desperation that go with that career path.

FAVORITE STORIES EXERCISE

Write about some of your favorite stories from when you were younger. Write about your memories of at least ten events in your life which you remember vividly. These stories should be about times you were happy and engaged. Where you were enjoying what you were doing.

When you have finished writing, review what you have written. See if there are any common themes. People, places, activities, or other elements that form a pattern. Look for commonalities related to why these events and stories resonate with you. Examine them to discover any purpose or passions that surface.

HOBBIES/INTERESTS

What were your hobbies and interests when you were younger? List your hobbies and interests. Do you see any patterns? Why these hobbies and interests, and not others? Do any of the hobbies or interests suggest a purpose or passions you had forgotten?

PEOPLE/IDEAS ATTRACTED TO

Another way to tease out your purpose and passions is to consider the people and ideas that interested you.

Who are were your favorite friends, teachers and public figures? Why? Look at those people and see if there were things they had in common. Were these people similar in any way?

If you find you were attracted to people with common interests or personalities, you may discover insights into your purpose or passions.

ADDITIONAL QUESTIONS

If you are still having trouble rediscovering you purpose and passions, or if you just want to consider them in a different way, **ask yourself these questions:**

- Why did you become a lawyer?

- What is your why now?

- Why do you get up in the morning?

- Why do you go to work?

- Why do you have your current job and career path?

- What is your definition of success?

Your answer to these questions will help you clarify your purpose and passions. They will help you identify the reasons for your current dissatisfaction. The answers will give you clues about potential jobs and career paths that will allow you to achieve success, prosperity, and personal fulfillment.

Think about these questions for the next few days. Do it while you're in the shower or taking a walk. Jot down your ideas. Your thoughts are valuable and will slip away if you don't write about them. Then, schedule some uninterrupted time to more fully write your answers to the questions and exercises.

Unless you know what is important to you on a deep level – your purpose and passions, your "why" – you will continue to be dissatisfied with your job and career path.

PRACTICAL PASSION

WHAT IS PRACTICAL PASSION?

I regularly see slogans like "follow your passion and success will follow" and "follow your passion and money will follow." These slogans are spouted by respected career experts and printed on tee-shirts. They are ubiquitous.

Unfortunately, this advice about passion, at least in a career context, is incomplete at best, and just plain wrong at worst.

In professional careers, the concept of passion must be refined. Passion is defined as an intense emotion. I may have an intense emotion — say, anger directed toward a kid bullying my daughter – but if I follow that passion and hit the bully, what will follow is not success or money, but a visit to the hospital or jail, and possibly both. The passion in your ideal career must be something positive, something related to serving other people.

Lawyers who are following their passion must focus that passion on a necessary and crucial corollary. That corollary is: "and your passion must be expressed as something other people want and will pay you to provide." I'm passionate about college football. But at this point in my life, I doubt I could build a career around it by creating a service others want and will pay me to provide.

The corollary – your passion must be expressed as something other people want and will pay you to provide – is what I refer to as practical passion. Practical passion is found where the activities you enjoy and the skills you excel at intersect with what other people want and will pay you to provide. Two elements are necessary for practical passion. Skills you excel at and activities you enjoy doing, and someone who will pay you to provide a service where you use those skills and activities.

USE ENTREPRENEURIAL MINDSET TO DISCOVER PRACTICAL PASSION

To discover your practical passion, identify the skills you both excel at and enjoy doing. The Inventory chapter includes questions and exercises to help you identify the skills you excel at. Use your knowledge and creativity to brainstorm ways you can use those skills and activities to offer services which other people want and will pay you to provide. This exercise is more powerful when done in collaboration with others – including mentors, mastermind groups, advisers, consultants, or coaches – than when trying to do it in isolation.

In today's world, lawyers are more like entrepreneurs or freelancers than traditional employees or partners. To create your ideal career and achieve success, prosperity, and personal fulfillment, you will need to think more like an entrepreneur than an employee. Use your entrepreneurial mindset to find ways to express your practical passion in your career.

If you continue with an employee mindset, you will limit your career opportunities. An employee mindset is fixed on doing whatever is necessary to further the goals of the employer in order to advance in the organization. An entrepreneurial mindset leads to action guided by practical passion. Your action is focused on your vision of the future. I should stress that an entrepreneurial lawyer working in an organizational environment must also take actions that will further the goals of the employer.

There are two essential differences between an entrepreneurial and an employee mindset. First, the entrepreneur is always looking for opportunities to express their passions in service of their employer or clients. To find their practical passion, even as an employee. Second, the entrepreneur leaves the employer much more quickly when they realize there's little room left for them to express their practical passion and engage in meaningful work.

The employee mindset is becoming less and less viable for a successful professional career. Today, if your services are not valued – whether the market is your firm, an employer, or comprises individual or corporate clients – you're in real trouble. Take control of your career by finding ways to express your practical passion. Use the skills you excel at in ways that interest you, and that other people will pay you to provide.

Traditionally, lawyers have been service providers. This has been true whether they were providing services to a firm, a corporate employer, or directly to an individual or business client. However, I am seeing more lawyers and law firms providing value by offering a product. They are transforming what was a service offering into a product. Consider whether there are products you can offer to others, either as complements to your primary service offerings or as a stand-alone source of revenue.

PURPOSE AND PASSION IN YOUR CURRENT JOB AND CAREER PATH

How will the knowledge about your purpose and passions help you revitalize your job and career? In two ways. It will help you focus on actions to take right now to improve your satisfaction with your current job. It will also help you in envisioning your ideal career.

REFOCUS YOUR CURRENT JOB

How do you incorporate your purpose and passions into your current job and life? By focusing on them and looking for opportunities to express your purpose and passions. Awareness and intention are the watchwords.

If one of your passions is helping others, seek opportunities to work with individuals instead of businesses. Even Big Law represents individuals. If representing individuals who can afford Big Law rates still doesn't stir your passions, pro bono work may be an alternative.

If your passion is adventure, but you are a deal jockey, seek work on deals that involve startups or cutting-edge ventures. If you're a litigator, seek high-risk and long-shot litigation projects.

Are you passionate about learning and knowledge? Write that book or article you've thought about for years. Find opportunities to explore different areas of law that interest you.

Take small actions now. These actions will improve your satisfaction with your current job as you continue to work through and implement your career revitalization process.

Identify work which is more engaging and in line with your purpose and passions. It will do wonders for your state of mind. You will be more energized. You will explore different work, clients, or ways to work. Some of these might not be a great fit. But some experiences, no matter how small, will lead to ideas about what your perfect job and ideal career path will look like.

While you are working on finding the perfect job and creating your ideal career, continue to explore opportunities to incorporate activities in line with your purpose and passion into your current work. Whether you get brownie points for your initiative or a stern rebuke for squandering billable time, you are moving toward the perfect job and ideal career.

REVISE YOUR CAREER PATH

In rediscovering your purpose and passions, you may realize, if you don't already know it, that following your purpose and passions will require more than refocusing on your current job. You will need to engage in a process of not only refocusing on your current job, but revising your career path, sometimes drastically.

The purpose and passions you identified are the basis for a process of envisioning your ideal career and life, as discussed in the next section. If you don't envision and create your ideal career path by incorporating your purpose and passions, your next job will be no better than your current job. While you may find a different job, you will be just as miserable, and possibly more so, than you are today. That's what happens to unhappy lawyers who jump at the next opportunity to switch firms, go in-house, or even leave the law. Without a well thought-out long-term career plan incorporating their purpose, passions, and vision, they continue to be dissatisfied with their careers.

Thoughts of practicality, student loans, lack of experience and connections, and negative reactions from family, friends, and colleagues may creep in. Ignore them for now. Those issues and others will be considered in time. But, if you let them intrude now, you will hinder your progress or even stop the process before it gets started.

If you are an unhappy lawyer who is overworked, stressed, bored, or depressed, you can continue on your current career path. That course will most likely lead to more of the same. Some lawyers take that route. You know a few. Not a pretty picture. It gets worse, not better, unless you take action to find the perfect job and create your ideal career.

Or, perhaps you've had enough misery. If so, read on and answer the questions and do the exercises in the next section to envision the perfect job and ideal career.

You have completed the exercises in this section to rediscover your purpose and passions. You have considered practical passion. You have looked at ways to incorporate purpose and passion into your job and career today. You are now ready to take the next step in the career revitalization process: envisioning your ideal career and life.

RE-VISIONING YOUR CAREER

Vision is related to your purpose and passions. Your vision is a distinct picture of how your purpose and passions will manifest themselves in your career. Your vision is a detailed picture of your career and life incorporating your purpose and passions.

YOUR VISION

What is your vision?

If your first answer to the question is to be rich and powerful, you need to dig deeper. While money and power may be goals, most people lose whatever passion they have if there's no purpose behind making the money or having the power. Lawyers whose visions of the future is focused only on money or power are usually empty and miserable, even if they have large incomes or exercise great power.

You have the power to find the perfect job and to create your ideal career. You can take action that is guided by your practical passion to create a career of success, prosperity, and personal fulfillment. However, laser focus is required.

What is the target of your laser focus? It is your vision of the perfect job and ideal career. This is a crucial concept in the career revitalization process. There are few "musts" within the career revitalization process, but this is one. The rest of the career revitalization process hinges on having a detailed vision of the perfect job and ideal career which you can focus on.

Envisioning your ideal career is not a one-time exercise. You will revisit this process regularly throughout your career. As you progress on your career path, your purpose and passions may evolve, and your experiences may lead to revisions of your envisioned perfect job and ideal career. While it's crucial to have a vision of your future to aim your focus toward, it's also crucial to periodically examine your vision and make adjustments as necessary.

CAREER VISIONING EXERCISES

You've rediscovered your purpose in life. Your passions are rising. How do you direct and focus those passions? By envisioning the perfect job and ideal career path within the context of your desired lifestyle.

You are now clear on your purpose and passions. It's time to channel your energy into envisioning how those elements will manifest in your career and life.

Career Visioning Exercise

Imagine your ideal career and life at three points: say, five years, fifteen years, and thirty years from today. This is the time to be open and non-judgmental. Let the ideas and images flow without censoring whether you think they are realistic.

What do you see? Be specific. Why are you doing what you envision? What are you doing in your job and life? Where are you doing it? What gives you pleasure and how do you measure success? Who are the people you are closest to in your family, local community, professional community, and life? What do you do for fun? Describe a typical day.

The more you can get into the picture of your life, the better. Envision seeing yourself and hearing people around you talking. Envision touching the objects around you. What aromas and tastes do you sense? This vision will have a significant impact on your career and life.

Write about your vision. Use stream of consciousness as your guide. Avoid using an eraser or editing your writing. Let it all out. Get it all down on paper.

The clearer your career vision is, the more useful it will be in your career transition process. The more specific, the better. Every sensory perception you have is vital.

In this step, it is important for you to get everything in your ideal career clearly specified. Don't filter yourself now. In later steps, you will prioritize and consider your vision through a more realistic lens. Not now. Let your imagination run wild.

Write about your vision. These questions may help you get started.

- What do you do during the day?

- Who are your clients?

- Who are your colleagues?

- Where are you during the day?

- What are you wearing?
- What are your clients' problems?
- What skills do you use to help solve your clients' problems?
- Do you sense any smells?
- What are your clients wearing?
- What do you see when you look around?
- How do you communicate with your clients?
- How much money do you make?
- What services or products do you offer?
- How do your clients find you?
- How are you compensated?
- What sounds do you hear?
- What do you do in the evenings?
- What do you do on the weekends?
- What tastes do you sense?
- Where do you live?
- What are your hobbies?
- What recreational activities do you participate in?
- What does your family look like?
- Who are your friends?
- What are your interests?
- How are your physical condition, nutrition, and sleep?

- What is most important to you?

- What items are close to you when you work?

Spend time with your vision of an ideal career and life sharply in focus, and write about everything that comes into your mind. Don't censor yourself. Just write.

Use the questions above to spark more thoughts.

Write about them.

This is an important step in the career revitalization process. Take it seriously.

YOUR CLIENTS

When you envision your career, two of the most crucial questions to answer concern your clients. First, who are your ideal clients? Second, what services do you offer to your ideal clients? These two questions are interrelated, but I will consider them separately in order to help clarify what you will look at during the process of envisioning the perfect job and ideal career.

Like all visioning exercises, you begin with a picture of the future in a perfect world with no limits or consideration of practicalities. Consideration of those potential constraints will come later.

Who Are Your Ideal Clients?

Envision what your ideal client looks like in detail. Who are the clients you serve in your career? What group of people do you want to help?

All lawyers serve other people. It doesn't matter whether you call these people your clients, customers, or employers. Lawyers who work within a firm, at a company, or in government have two sets of clients they serve. They serve their employers and their employers' clients. If you work within an organization, **there are two questions to answer when envisioning your clients:**

- Who are your ideal clients and

- What is the perfect organization within which to serve those clients?

Imagine the perfect job. Who would you be working with every day? Will your clients be retaining you for personal or business issues? Will your clients be individuals or representatives of an organization? If the ideal clients are organizations, at what level within the organization are the people who you deal with regularly?

In answering these questions, remember the people you like to be around in both work and play. Consider the personality traits of your ideal clients. Are your clients easy-going, driven, smart, empathetic, compassionate, young, or old? What motivates your ideal clients? Money, power, prestige, justice, or social responsibility? Or, something else?

If you are in the earlier stages of your career, you may not know people who you believe will be your ideal clients. Find out as much as you can about the people you envision being your ideal clients. Talk to lawyers who work with these clients. Use your personal network to arrange meetings with people you envision as ideal clients.

Is your ideal client an organization? Then you also need to consider the culture of the organizations you envision as ideal clients. The culture and people who work within investment banks differ significantly from the culture and people who work with non-profits or the government.

Your goal is to be detailed and concrete when you envision your ideal clients – both in terms of your ultimate clients and the organization you work within to serve those clients.

How Will You Serve Your Ideal Clients?

Once you envision your ideal clients, you need to envision what you will do for them. What problems will you be helping them solve? What services will you be offering to these clients?

These may be hard questions to answer, but they must be answered in order for you to move forward intentionally to find the perfect job and create your ideal career. If you are early in your career, you might need to do more research to determine the problems of your ideal clients. You will also have to research the services they want you to offer in order to help them solve those problems. Even if you are well-along on your career path, a thorough consideration of ideal clients' problems and the services needed to solve those problems can be an enlightening experience.

Taking this perspective of envisioning the perfect job and ideal career is unusual for many lawyers. The usual approach is to showcase your skills and experience. Then you try to convince a potential client, whether it is an employer or the ultimate client, that they need what you offer. The focus is on you, not the client.

Approach your job and career as a business with the mindset of an entrepreneur and the attitude of a consultant. Focus on the ideal client and their problems. For some lawyers, it may be a subtle change from "what you have that a client needs" to "what a client needs that you have." For others, it will be a sea change. From "I'm the professional and know what my clients need — me" to the realization that clients know their business and problems. Clients engage lawyers who collaborate with them to solve their problems.

Perfect jobs and ideal careers are built on knowing your ideal client and how you will solve their problems. But, the most important factor in whether you find the perfect job and create your ideal career is whether you are following your passions and interests. You may have the skills and experience to serve clients and help them solve their problems. But, if you have no passion or little interest in your work or for your clients, you will be miserable. Even if you are paid handsomely.

You may be temporarily satisfied with having a job and making a good living doing something for which you have no passion and little interest. But, it is not a long-term formula for success, prosperity, and personal fulfillment. Many lawyers considered successful and prosperous are dying inside. You want to feel successful, prosperous, and personally fulfilled. You'll feel this way when your clients and the work you do for them is aligned not only with your skills and experience, but with your passions and interests.

FAMILY, FRIENDS, AND COLLEAGUES IN DISTRESSED CAREER REVITALIZATIONS

When revitalizing your distressed career, you must consider the reaction of your family, friends, and colleagues. However, it is best to wait until you clearly understand your purpose, passions and vision before fully sharing them with many people.

It is wise to get input and receive support from a spouse before you begin the career revitalization process. You must have your spouse's support before finalizing your vision of the perfect job and ideal career. When your vision may cause an immediate decrease in income, fear may dominate your spouse's response, and resistance could be substantial. The support of a spouse is crucial; otherwise, the relationship may not survive. Your spouse is the one person you must talk to before you finalize your vision of the perfect job and ideal career.

Family members, friends, and colleagues will react to your vision for your career from their own perspectives. Their reactions may come out of their fears or out of their hope and support for you. The bigger the distance between your current career path and your envisioned ideal career path, the more strident the opposition is likely to be.

It is crucial to have a clear vision of your ideal career firmly in place before sharing it with too many people. You also need to prepare for and plan how to respond to negative reactions from family, friends, and colleagues. Listen attentively to their reactions. They may share perspectives that are helpful. But, you must be prepared to stand firm for what you believe is the perfect job and ideal career path.

Assess the reaction of your family, friends, and colleagues. It will help you to identify those people you can count on for support and encouragement. Support and encouragement may sometimes be in short supply while you are revitalizing your distressed career. Know those people who you can depend on for their support and encouragement before you implement your vision.

CHAPTER 4

INVENTORY (STRENGTHS & INTERESTS)

INVENTORY IN DISTRESSED BUSINESSES

Corporate turnaround professionals evaluate management at the beginning of an engagement. Reviews of each member of the management team are comprehensive. What are the individuals' knowledge levels, skills, and strengths? The turnaround professionals must know what they are working with in the turnaround process. They want an accurate measure of the inventory of the business. An inventory in the broadest sense. Not just an inventory of the goods available for sale, raw materials, and the equipment. They also want an inventory of the human capital. The skills of the people in the organization, from the executives down to the hourly employees. In a service business, human capital is the most valuable item in the business's inventory.

Unless there is an accurate inventory, corporate turnaround professionals don't know what resources there are to work with in the revitalization process. One thing they often discover is that the inventory is inaccurate and out of date. Service offerings or products that are not attractive to the company's market, and employees whose skill sets are out of date, are useless in the revitalization process. Until the inventory is measured, the turnaround professionals are working with one hand tied behind their backs.

INVENTORY IN YOUR DISTRESSED CAREER

In revitalizing your distressed career, you need to conduct a thorough inventory of your knowledge, skills, interests and personality. When you appreciate your strengths and weaknesses, you can create a strategic plan to find the perfect job and create your ideal career.

CURRENT EMPLOYMENT STATUS

You must get real, and real quick. Brutal honesty with yourself is crucial at this stage of the career revitalization process.

WHAT IS YOUR EMPLOYMENT STATUS?

This seems like a simple question. You are employed or unemployed. Name of the firm, rank, and serial number. Next. Not so fast.

If you're employed, your biggest insights from answering this question will come from looking at your employer and considering its future. Not by taking a quick look at the current Am Law 200 or Fortune 500 rankings, but by examining how prepared the firm and its leaders are for the future. Your future.

You must also do the same analysis in relation to your practice group. How stable are the group and its leaders within the firm? Is your practice area growing or contracting? Are new competitors, either traditional firms or alternative service providers, competing for your practice area's client base? What are the prospects for the industries your practice group serves?

A critical evaluation of your firm and practice group requires knowledge of the legal industry. Reasoned judgments about the future of the legal industry and your practice area are also necessary. Read leading legal commentators like Bruce MacEwen (aka. Adam Smith, Esq.) and Richard Susskind to get a feel for the future of the legal industry.

Do you see a clear path for your career at your current firm? What obstacles do you face on your current career path? What is the realistic probability of getting to your desired level within the firm? Remember, brutal honesty and not optimistic hope is required in order for your answer to be useful in the career revitalization process.

One last question. This is important! Do you want to be on your current career path in the first place?

If you are not employed, doing this analysis for your last employer will enlighten you. You can use the exercise as a post-mortem and learn a few lessons.

WHAT'S WORKING/GOOD

It's important for lawyers with distressed careers experiencing pain or fear to recognize and acknowledge the positive aspects of their current situation. Even if you are unemployed, you have an advanced degree and some experience. If you are employed, you have a job and an income. Even if you are overwhelmed and stressed, you are gaining valuable experience.

It is also helpful to be grateful for the good things in your life. Relationships with family, friends, and colleagues. Skills you excel at performing and which you enjoy. Personality traits that make your life and the lives of others better.

There may be tough periods to face when creating your ideal career. Especially if a crisis or contentious issues with your current employer have prompted your desire to implement the career revitalization process.

Acknowledge what is good in your life. Focusing on what is working and who your supporters are will help you have gratitude for the good things in your life. Recent research has found that gratitude is an emotion closely correlated with happiness. Until you can work through the career revitalization process, focusing on what is good in your life and being grateful may help you be happier in your current situation.

PRESSING CRITICAL CHALLENGES

Focus on the positive aspects of your career and life. However, you must also acknowledge and address pressing critical challenges in your career and life. If you are not working, are facing serious health issues, or are going through a divorce, your career revitalization process will face special challenges. You will compromise the process of finding the perfect job and creating your ideal career if these serious issues are not addressed.

If you are not working and face financial pressures, you may need to find a job quickly to produce an income. Even if you take a less-than-perfect job to relieve financial pressures, though, you can do it in a strategic way, following the principles of the career revitalization process. Consider not only the income available, but also how any aspect of the job can serve your long-term goals.

If you need to take a contract position doing document discovery, do it strategically. Is there a position available at a firm or company you may be interested in exploring? How about a project in an industry that may be of interest? Or, a project using software or processes you would like to learn more about?

Small decisions can produce big results on your career path. Many lawyers who make seemingly insignificant choices about relatively unimportant matters look back after a few years and realize these small decisions had a significant impact on their career path.

If you are confronting a serious health issue, possibly caused by the stress of your job, address it now. If you are not in good health, your career revitalization process will be hindered. Go to a qualified medical professional and take the advice you are given. If the advice is to take medication, take the medication. If it is to get more exercise, eat better, sleep more, drink less, or meditate, do it. The better your body is functioning, the more good clean energy you can devote to finding the perfect job and creating your ideal career. And, the less you will be restrained by having to address health issues on an ad hoc basis at inopportune times.

Is a relationship with a spouse, child, or other family member causing you pain and capturing your attention and focus? Are your job search and career revitalization efforts an attempt to help resolve these issues? Or, is a relationship with your spouse or partner broken and irreparable, to where a separation or divorce is unavoidable? If the relationship is not repairable, the issue must be addressed and resolved. While feeling the weight of the problem, your efforts in your career revitalization process will be less than optimal.

Acknowledge and resolve critical challenges with unemployment, health issues, or relationship problems. It is not only necessary, but it will allow you to focus on finding the perfect job and creating your ideal career.

360-DEGREE ASSESSMENT

You see yourself in a certain way. Sometimes that matches how the world sees you. Other times, not so much.

One of the best exercises you can do to get an accurate view of yourself is a 360-degree evaluation. This process provides a clear view of your career from many perspectives. By going through this exercise, you will get a picture of yourself from many angles.

A 360-degree evaluation is a process where people from different areas of your life provide an evaluation. You ask your colleagues, partners, associates, staff, clients, friends, and family to evaluate you. They provide their impressions of your work, skills, and personality traits, and any other information that may be useful for you to get a better perspective on how others see you.

The feedback and information obtained in a 360-degree evaluation is invaluable in helping you identify your strengths and weaknesses. It gives you information you can use later in building your personal brand, one of the key elements of the career revitalization process. The 360-evaluation may be uncomfortable, but sometimes it takes bitter medicine to cure the patient.

CAREER

You need an unbiased evaluation of your current career. Total objectivity. No holding back.

The best way to evaluate your career is to ask for honest feedback from people you work with every day. People above and below you. Your clients. Even close professional acquaintances at other firms.

Lawyers are resistant to evaluations, as most people are. We are risk-adverse and don't want to hear negative feedback. We don't like to ask questions we don't already know the answer to (remnants of Moot Court or Trail Advocacy), and we're pessimistic and expect the worst. And, what if the evaluation is none too complimentary? We need to hear that in the worst way.

My experience, both personally and with many other people going through an evaluation process, is that we don't see ourselves as clearly as we think we do. Some of us overstate our positive qualities and strengths, and understate our negative qualities and weaknesses. Some of us are just the opposite. We don't know our strengths and think we are weak in many areas. Whichever camp you fall into, your own evaluation of yourself may not to match the evaluators' judgments in many respects.

If you're lucky, you've been through a recent comprehensive evaluation process. Go back and reconsider the feedback and comments with an open mind. Try to learn, not defend or rationalize.

Whether you have been through a recent evaluation or not, ask partners and associates you work with to give you a quick evaluation. Ask support staff. Ask your clients. **The following is a short list of open-ended questions you can ask.**

- What is your general impression of me?

- What do you believe my strengths are?

- What do you believe I could do better?

- What are my best personality traits?

- What are the personality traits I could work on?

Ask in person or by email. Explain that you are trying to get a better idea of your strengths and weaknesses, and of personality traits that ingratiate you with others or put up a wall of separation. The key is to be sincere in your requests, ask others to be forthright, and not take too much of their time for the evaluation.

Give people a way to provide evaluations anonymously if desired. Follow up with a thank-you to everyone, even those who don't participate.

You may also want a more thorough evaluation from a few key people in your office. Schedule a time when you are both able to be fully present. The meeting should be outside of the office. In the conversation, probe areas critical to your career advancement. You need not be defensive or offer an explanation. Just listen and ask probing questions.

Many law firms are terrible at evaluations. The evaluators don't like to do them. Lawyers worry that their assessments of others could be used against them, and so they don't like to take definitive positions, especially if their assessment is positive. They don't want such an evaluation to come back and haunt them if you don't advance at a typical pace.

As a complement to your evaluation process, consider hiring a consultant to assist you. A consultant can be a buffer between you and others in asking probing questions and getting honest feedback. Many lawyers will be reluctant to participate in these interviews, and for the same reasons that they are hesitant to give direct feedback in an evaluation. If you aren't able to get an outside consultant to help with the evaluations, sit down with an expert and review your prior evaluations. An expert adds unbiased perspective. They will help you decode words or meanings in the evaluations, which you could otherwise misinterpret.

Many lawyers worry about asking for feedback outside of a formal process. They fear the request will be taken negatively and will harm their opportunity for advancement. But what's the harm? If the lawyers you work with, and who are responsible for your career advancement, are unwilling to give you feed-back, there may already be a problem.

Are you satisfied with working for months or years without being evaluated? Since you are likely a poor evaluator of your skills, how do you gauge whether you are leading with your strengths? How do you uncover your weaknesses?

Everyone is busy, and few lawyers want to give negative feedback that may affect their working relationships. But, if you don't get feedback and evaluations, you've lost valuable infor-mation to help you take control of your career and get the most out of your career revitalization process.

PERSONAL LIFE

While it may be useful to separate your work from the rest of your life, the elements are intertwined.

Career issues can turn into personal problems, and personal problems can turn into career issues. We all have colleagues who lost their spouse to divorce because they spent so much time focusing on their careers. We also have colleagues whose personal relationships, health, or financial issues have adverse-ly affected their careers.

In revitalizing your career as an entrepreneurial business, you must consider your personal life as well as your career.

Health And Relationships

Health issues can compromise your ability, energy, and mo-tivation to revitalize your career and rejuvenate your life. Is your job causing health problems? I suspect you are not getting enough sleep. Are you keeping physically fit and maintaining healthy eating habits? How are you managing stress? If you haven't had an exam in the past year, schedule one today.

Evaluate your mental, emotional, and spiritual health for a complete picture. Be honest with yourself, and solicit feedback from close family members and friends.

Your relationships will provide much-needed support for your efforts to revitalize your career. But, relationship issues can torpedo your efforts to find the perfect job and create your ideal career.

After our health, our relationships are the most important factor in a satisfying and well-lived life. Do you have a life partner? Are they supportive? What are their views on your current job and possible career paths? Can you count on family and friends to support you emotionally?

How is your relationship with your spouse?

If there are chronic unresolved issues with family members, the emotional stress around these matters can hinder or derail progress in other areas of your life. I am not a therapist, but from personal experience, I appreciate that using the services of a skilled therapist can be beneficial in coping with such a situation.

How broad are your personal and professional networks? How strong are the relationships? Has it been a while (or ages) since you connected with them?

Review and update your contact list. This will help you get a better idea of the current breadth and depth of your network.

FINANCES

The American Bar Association reports that as of 2012, the average law school debt of public law school graduates was $84,000, and for private law school graduates it was $122,158. The New America Foundation recently reported that the average indebtedness of law graduates increased by more than $50,000 between 2004 and 2012. A typical law student has $140,000 in educational debt.

Even if you are one of the fortunate lawyers without educational debt, you need a detailed account of your finances. You need to be clear on your current financial situation before creating your strategic and action plans to realize your vision, find the perfect job, and create your ideal career. Otherwise, you may discover financial constraints which are difficult to overcome. If you are clear on your financial status before you plan and implement your career revitalization, it is much easier to devise plans to address and surmount financial constraints.

Answering the following questions will help you better appreciate your financial situation.

Income

- Can you sustain your current lifestyle on your present income?
- What income do you need to support your current lifestyle?
- What income do you need to support your desired future lifestyle?
- How stable is your income?
- Does your spouse produce an income?

Expenses

- Do you have a budget?

- What are your fixed expenses?

- How long can you cover the expenses of your current life-style with no income?

- Is it possible to cut some of your discretionary expenses?

Debts & Assets

- How much is your school, mortgage, auto, and credit card debt, combined?

- What is the minimum monthly amount needed to service the debt?

- Have you explored alternative debt repayment scenarios?

- Do you have any savings or investments?

- Do you have assets you can sell to raise cash?

- If you have a spouse, do they have debts or assets?

Your current and desired future lifestyles are important factors to consider in envisioning your ideal career. Financial matters may limit you, but they might not be as constraining as you fear.

Once you get a detailed account of your current financial status, it is necessary to evaluate different financial scenarios based on your envisioned lifestyle. What amount of income do you need for the envisioned lifestyle? Don't forget that you will also need to save some of the income for your children's educational expenses and your retirement.

STRENGTHS & INTERESTS

Focus on your strengths. They are a core pillar of your career revitalization. Your strengths are the building blocks for creating your personal brand. Your personal brand is the foundation you build on to find the perfect job and create your ideal career.

Consider both your strengths and your weaknesses. Every great hero has strengths and weaknesses. The driving force of the hero's journey is in overcoming their weaknesses by using their strengths to deal with adversity.

Many career experts will tell you to work on developing skills in areas where you are weak. That advice is wrong and harmful for most lawyers. Most likely, your weaknesses are in areas that do not interest you. Why spend the time and effort to be more skilled in an area that doesn't interest you?

In today's world, there are many resources available to assist you in your weak areas, or in areas which you aren't interested in. You can always compensate for skills you are weak in or for activities you don't like to do. In the large firm or corporate world, you can identify colleagues or support staff to collaborate with while you are using your own strengths to follow your practical passion. In the small business or entrepreneurial world, you can collaborate with other professionals or use virtual assistants to cover your weak skills or complete tasks that don't interest you.

It is critical to highlight your strengths and the activities that interest you. Recognize those strengths and activities will be the foundation of the action you take to express your practical passion and to find the perfect job and create your ideal career.

WHAT ARE YOUR STRENGTHS?

Your evaluation of your strengths might be skewed or inaccurate. The evaluations you received in doing the work in the previous section gave you a good place to start your analysis. If you haven't gone through the full evaluation exercises, ask a few colleagues, friends, and family members to give you their evaluation of your strengths.

Your strengths include your knowledge, skills, and personality. Look at all your strengths, not just your technical knowledge and practice skills. Personal qualities, including social and emotional intelligence, are important. How do you rate?

Your legal knowledge is what you learned in law school and in your experience practicing law. It includes your general legal knowledge and your specialty practice knowledge. Knowledge about particular industries, types of clients, or technologies and skills outside the law are also significant strengths.

Your non-legal knowledge acquired during other phases of your formal education, in non-legal jobs and volunteer experiences, and through hobbies and other interests you had matter as well.

The last area to consider in inventorying your strengths is your personality. In many respects, personality skills – or traits where you are strong – are one of the most important factors to consider in finding the perfect job and creating your ideal career.

KNOWLEDGE

Knowledge is the foundation for your skills and interests. The more you know about a particular subject, the higher your potential skill level. As your knowledge increases, your interest may either increase or decrease.

You know specific areas of the law. You may be knowledgeable about civil procedure or criminal law. You may know more about commercial real estate than bankruptcy law. Or, you might know more about contracts than you do about torts.

You also know about industries outside of the law. This industry-specific knowledge has become much more important to clients over the past few years. You may be knowledgeable about venture capital or financial markets. Or, about the construction or transportation industries. Or, you might know more about software than you do about aerospace.

You learned about many other subjects while you were growing up, going to school, and working in your prior jobs. Everyone has their own unique body of knowledge.

What knowledge do you have? Categorize your knowledge. List areas where you are knowledgeable. What areas of legal practice do you specialize in? What industries or type of clients do you know well? What specific knowledge did you gain during your formal education? What knowledge did you acquire outside of your formal education or career?

The previous questions should stimulate thought. They will allow you to inventory all of your knowledge, including some you may have forgotten about or don't consider as relevant to your career at this stage. Don't censor yourself or be modest in this exercise. This is about gathering information. You will put it all together and see how it applies to creating your ideal career later in the career revitalization process.

Knowledge may provide personal fulfillment, but knowledge alone cannot propel you to success or prosperity. That is a hard truth experienced by many newly-minted graduates of law and business schools, as well as some lawyers fairly far along in their careers.

SKILLS

Your strengths also include your skills. Now that you have a list of all the areas where you are knowledgeable, it's time to focus on the skills you possess. Skills are the practical application of knowledge. You might be knowledgeable about civil procedure, but do you know how to draft a Motion to Dismiss? Knowledge is knowing, and skills are doing. Skills are applied knowledge.

While being knowledgeable about something is great and can be its own reward, employers and clients are interested in your skills. They want to know if you can do something, not just talk about it in a knowing way. This is the major disconnect between graduating law students and their first employer. While the students have knowledge in many areas of the law, and more in some areas than senior partners, many of these same students have few practical legal skills. And it's the skills that employers and the ultimate client desire and pay you to provide.

Review your list of knowledge. Do this for both legal areas and non-legal areas.

Then consider whether you have skills that may be outside of your areas of knowledge. You may not consider yourself knowledgeable about negotiation, but you can negotiate a real estate deal. You may not consider yourself knowledgeable about cooking, but you can host a cook-out for fifty people.

Be thorough in this exercise. You may uncover long-forgotten skills that might be significant in creating your ideal career.

Make a list of all the professional areas where you have above-average skills. From taking depositions to drafting a motion for change of venue to getting a zoning variance. List specific skills in the different areas where you are knowledgeable.

Add to your list by including non-legal skills like working with pivot tables in Excel, constructing a WordPress site, or making a PowerPoint deck.

Include non-work skills you've learned in other occupations. Even include current or former hobbies such as catching fish, hosting a dinner party for 30 people, or climbing tall mountain peaks.

Then rank your skills by how highly you excel in performing the skill. Make a list of your top twenty-five skills.

Interests

Your career takes much of your time and energy. While you can succeed in jobs or on a career path that doesn't interest you, you will not prosper or be personally fulfilled. No matter how successful you appear to the outside world, if you don't feel prosperous or personally fulfilled in your career, you will never be satisfied, content, or happy. No matter how well you do your job or how knowledgeable and skillful you might be, if what you do doesn't interest you, prosperity and personal fulfillment will be beyond your grasp. The legal industry is full of lawyers who appear successful and even prosperous, but who are not fulfilled and are miserable. Do you want to be one of those lawyers?

Make a list of all your interests. What interests you about the jobs you've had? What did you like to do? What were you doing when you had those periods when you were in the flow of work and lost track of time? Don't limit this exercise to your legal jobs. Examine your non-legal jobs. Look back at your interests in your life. What subjects interested you in school? What hobbies have you had in your life?

Once you prepare a comprehensive list of your interests, see if there's any pattern to them. Do some fit well within a broader group? Are certain skills used to engage with those interests? Do your interests come and go, or have they remained consistent?

Rank your interests according to what is most interesting to you now. If you had completed this exercise five years ago, would the list be similar? Or, is your pattern to continually develop interests where you are fixated on one for a while, and then move on to other areas of interest? If your interests are stable and constant, you will likely be fulfilled in a job that allows you to work in those areas of interest. If your interests are evolving, you need to find jobs that allow for that evolution. Or, realize that you may be someone who will change jobs on a more regular basis than the average lawyer.

Rank your skills by your interest in using the skill. Compare this list with the list ranking the skills you excel at to find where your strengths and interests coincide. Make a third list with your top fifteen skills on a combined strength/interest scale.

PERSONAL TRAITS

A big factor in whether you are successful, prosperous, and personally fulfilled is whether the work you do is a good fit with your personality traits.

This analysis has nothing to do with good or bad. We each have different personalities. An introvert may function successfully as a trial litigator, but may not be happy doing it. An extrovert may be a successful tax lawyer, but will not be overjoyed with researching tax codes and regulations, and analyzing deal structures in agonizing detail. While playing against their type, such as an extroverted tax lawyer, may work for some lawyers, it is not a recipe for happiness at work or for personal fulfillment.

While you may be more astute in analyzing your personality traits than some of your other strengths, it is helpful for others to assist you in this analysis. In evaluating your personality traits, family and friends are at least as important as professional colleagues for soliciting feedback. You may have been acting in a role in your professional life for so long that you can't see that the behavior is not one of your natural strengths. You may have developed that trait where it is now a part of who you are. But, if you are still acting the part it may be a source of discomfort for you.

If you are having trouble identifying your strong personality traits, and don't feel you have the clarity you need, consider using one of the commercial personality assessments. Using a commercial personality assessment might also be appropriate if you don't feel that your personality is the best fit for your current practice area.

In evaluating your personality, you want to examine who you are as a person. The real you without your professional persona. The more aligned your personal and professional personas, the less friction and discomfort you will have in your life.

By the time we are in our professional careers, it's hard to change our personality traits. It is important for us to appreciate our traits, both the positive and negative traits, so we can emphasize or moderate them where appropriate. But, we are unlikely to change the traits without consistent, intentional practice. Most of us will not be prepared to do this work unless the trait is severely limiting our professional career. If that is your situation, consulting a therapist or other professional might be appropriate.

Some lawyers grapple with acknowledging and accepting who they are with their unique personalities. Once they have a clear perspective of themselves, they should consider how well their personalities fit with their work. How does the work you do, where you do it, and your colleagues and clients fit with your personality?

Consider what type of law or function will fit your personality best. A lawyer who does not like conflict and confrontation may be a better fit in the role of a tax planning lawyer than that of a front-line litigator. A lawyer quick on their feet may enjoy being a trial lawyer.

If you've been practicing law for a few years, you most likely know whether your practice fits your personality. I hope there is close alignment. You may benefit from looking at the different functions in your practice that are the best fits for your personality, and focusing your work in those areas. You can collaborate with others in work that matches their personality strengths to complement yours.

What if you find yourself in a practice area that does not match your personality? If you can't find a skill or function that fits your personality in your practice area, you need to consider retooling your practice to other areas. This may be difficult and take time, but if it puts you on your ideal career path, it will be worth the effort.

My divorce lawyer, who specialized in the emerging collaborative divorce area, once had a white collar criminal practice. His personality seemed to fit the collaborative divorce practice much better.

Consider where you practice. Are you in Big Law or a solo practitioner? Is your office in the central business area of a large city or in the suburbs of a smaller town? Are you an in-house lawyer or do you work within the government?

Your personality will fit better in some organizations than others. Different personality types gravitate to different settings. Driven, achievement-oriented lawyers who value high incomes are drawn to Big Law while purpose-oriented, collaborative lawyers are drawn to the government or public interest settings. If you are not practicing in an area aligned with your personality, you may be moving away from your ideal career path and setting yourself up for big problems.

Your colleagues and clients, the people you work with regularly, should be aligned with your personality. The clients of white shoe law firms and those of legal aid organizations are very different. The difference is not only in the law being practiced or where the practice is located; it is a different client personality. The personalities of your colleagues will also vary in different organizations. Some lawyers will be fulfilled by working with one organization, and other lawyers will be much happier working with another. To each their own. And if you are working with your ideal clients and colleagues, you will be much happier.

CHAPTER 5

RESEARCH AND DEVELOPMENT (CLARITY & FOCUS)

Corporate turnaround professionals evaluate the research and development function of distressed businesses for two reasons.

First, they want to know if any new services are in the pipeline. Are there potential new offerings to help solve clients' problems and generate revenue? How long will it be until services in the pipeline will be ready to offer to the public?

Second, the restructuring professionals want to determine what research and development efforts to focus on. In many distressed businesses, research and development work has been curtailed to cut expenses since the work doesn't lead to revenue in the short-term. But, lack of research and development can restrict a business's prospects over the long-term.

At this point in your career revitalization process, you have identified your purpose, passions, strengths, and interests. You have envisioned the perfect job and your ideal career. Now, it's time to do the research and development work. You will discover how and where all this fits together so you can find the perfect job and create your ideal career.

In these sections, you will consider the specifics and details about what you will do and in what environment, and where, and for whom? This is the time in your career revitalization process where the preparatory work leads to discovery of actual types of jobs, environments, locations, and employers. You are looking for the best fit with your priorities.

INFORMATION GATHERING

Are you anxious about the future of the legal industry?

Do you fear your job and career will suffer because of the changes in the legal industry?

Would you like to anticipate and judge how developments in the legal industry will affect your future?

-or-

Are you curious and intrigued by the evolution of the legal industry?

Do you find the opportunities created by disruptions in the industry exciting?

Would you like to be "in the know" and prepared to revise your career path as necessary to be at the top of your chosen field?

Either way, I have a simple solution for you. It will require a little upfront work. But I will show you how to minimize the time and effort you need to spend in order to stay abreast of trends in the legal industry or any other area.

Before I reveal this little secret, let me respond to some of your concerns.

A lawyer's first response to most things requiring a little work is that they don't have time. That's fine – understood. But if you don't make time now to consider the future of law, the future of your career might allow you plenty of time later.

Yep, the future is unpredictable. You're right. So, oh well, let's just get back to drafting confidentiality agreements or motions to dismiss. No use wasting billable time trying to see into the future.

Well, be ready for the future to smack your career into oblivion.

The future is unpredictable, but you can make educated predictions based on current information. Isn't that what lawyers do for a living? Is that deal going to close, or is that case going to settle?

To prepare for a successful career as a lawyer, either in or out of the law, you must know what is happening now and how that might affect your future. Listen to knowledgeable commentators on the future of law and then make your judgments about how to manage your career. But, how do you do this?

Identify good sources of information and commentary on the future of the legal industry. Most information is on the internet. Even the good stuff behind paywalls or in proprietary databases can be accessed in summary form by reading posts, articles, and reports by bloggers, journalists, and organizations. When you read something online that is useful, knowledgeable, and trustworthy, make note of the author and source.

HOW TO MAKE YOUR CRYSTAL BALL PROCESS EASY AND EFFICIENT

Many websites and blogs allow you to subscribe to feeds of blog posts or other regularly updated information. When you subscribe, any new posts or articles are sent to an RSS reader when published. You will need an RSS reader to access your subscriptions. I find Feedly to be the best of the readers, but other good ones are available. Feedly is free and easy to set up.

When you find a site that is a good source of information, click on the RSS symbol. It will be on the right side of the address bar of the site. That site will then be added to your Feedly. The RSS link is also sometimes placed near the social media buttons on the page. As an extra-special bonus, see my curated collections of Feedly subscriptions at: http://feedly.com/GregYates-Consulting. You can click on the feeds you want to subscribe to, and they will be added to your Feedly. Immediate gratification.

Couldn't you just subscribe to a site's newsletter or other email notification system? Sure, if your inbox isn't already full, go right ahead.

The more efficient tactic is to check all newsletters in your inbox and determine if there are RSS feeds for those newsletters. If so, subscribe to those feeds and direct them to your Feedly account. Then unsubscribe from the newsletter. I've just helped you with one of life's annoyances – an overflowing inbox. That's another bonus here, no thanks needed. I'm all about sharing information to make your career and life more enjoyable.

Now, set up a Pocket account.

Pocket allows you to read specific posts or articles from your RSS feed at your convenience. If you see something interesting when scrolling through your RSS subscriptions on Feedly, send it to Pocket so you can read it later. When you find other interesting pages on the internet, you can also send them to Pocket.

Pocket is free to use, although there is a paid option with more features. The free version is fine for most lawyers. You can add tags to organize the posts and articles for later reference. Pocket also has apps you can use to read saved items on your cell phone or tablet even if you are offline. There's also a search function, and you can archive items after you have read them.

Your "Future of Law" crystal ball system in a nutshell. Identify websites and blogs with good, trustworthy sources of recurring information about the future of law, or any other subject. Subscribe to the RSS feeds by sending them to Feedly. Review the posts in Feedly when you have a few minutes. Send the items you want to read later to Pocket. Read the items in Pocket at your leisure. That's it. You will soon develop a better idea about the future of law and how it will affect your career. A good payoff for a little work to set up your customized crystal ball system.

FUNCTIONS AND SKILLS

What will you be doing for the rest of your career? What functions will you be performing? What skills will you be using?

Research the functional aspect of your envisioned perfect job from one of two angles. Identify particular jobs you have an interest in and then find out what the key functions and skills are in those jobs. Or, focus on the skills you excel at and are interested in, and research jobs and careers where those skills are a major asset. Early in your career, you're more likely to take the former approach. If you are more experienced, you will take the latter approach.

Your research should be broad at first. Be creative. Go down a few roads less traveled in exploring a match between potential jobs and the skills you excel at and have an interest in using in your work. You will reach some dead-ends. This is much better than limiting your research to find the perfect job.

Remember who your ideal clients are in the perfect job. What will you be doing for your envisioned ideal clients against the backdrop of your skills, interests, and experience? The services you offer to your ideal clients will be based on your skills, interests, and experiences.

Research a few job categories that seem interesting. Drill deep to find out more about those jobs and the skills required. This will require not only research on the internet, but also talking to people with personal knowledge and experience in those areas. As you have most likely already encountered, written job descriptions can differ significantly from the actual jobs.

In finding jobs on your ideal career path, the skills you need to learn and the experiences you need to acquire are important factors to examine. The perfect job now may not be the one that produces the most income or has the most prestige. Instead, it may be a job where you can develop critical skills and get experiences to better serve your future clients. Remember your ideal client as you consider various jobs. Do this so you can acquire the skills and experience to serve those ideal clients, both now and in the future.

The functions you perform and the corresponding skills may change as you climb the career ladder. Research not only the functions and skills for your next job, but also the functions performed and the skills required for work you want to do later in your ideal career. This is where a significant disconnection occurs in many lawyers' careers.

As you advance in your career, you develop skills you excel at in a particular area. You are an expert. But, you may find yourself stuck in a senior-level associate position, managing lower level associates doing the work. It is an unfortunate position to be in if you want to advance further in your career. You are no longer doing the work you want to and using the skills you excel at performing. That work is now done by less experienced lawyers; you are managing them. And, you don't have the skills, or maybe even the interest, to move up to being the partner interacting with the general counsel of the clients. Your career path is at a dead-end, and you aren't even doing the work you like and for which you have skills you excel at performing.

Many lawyers get frustrated or depressed when they realize that the skills that got them to a certain level will not take them to a higher level. The excellent technical skills of a highly regarded 7th-year associate will not get you to equity partnership. Lawyers with just adequate technical skills as a 7th-year associate may have other skills that make them much stronger candidates for equity partnership.

It is crucial to know the functions and essential skills for the jobs on your ideal career path. Many law firms have become much better at specifying the technical skills of legal practice required at each level. What is still lacking and shrouded in mystery are the functions and skills to move beyond being a mid-level associate. In a recent survey of associates and legal professional development experts, only 54% of associates and 22% of professional development experts believed associates know what they need to do to advance in their careers. Most law firms must believe those best suited to being equity partners will "figure it out" and that the cream will rise to the top.

If you are still climbing the law firm ladder, or want to do so, you better figure it out sooner rather than later. You need to know what functions are valued and what skills are necessary for the most senior positions on your ideal career path. Can you perform those functions, and do you have those skills, or are you developing them through the experience you are getting? Most important, are they functions you like to do and skills you like to use?

At the top levels of almost all legal careers, getting clients and expanding the services which those clients buy are the most prized and rewarded functions. Functions traditionally thought of as marketing and sales. You might say, "wait a minute – is Yates crazy? The marketing department at my firm is not a well-regarded or well-paid area." You're right, but look at the highest paid partners in your firm. If you can get an accurate glimpse into their work and lives, you'll discover that much of their time is spent in marketing or sales efforts.

TARGET MARKETS

Which industry or industries are you going to serve? Which industries do you have the most knowledge of and experience in? Which industries have problems you can solve?

What's your target market? A target market is the group of employers or clients you focus your time, effort, and energy on to find a job or clients.

Whether you are providing outside legal services, being an in-house counsel, or offering other related legal or non-legal services, most lawyers start with too broad a target market. Many litigators think they can win any case, and many transactional lawyers believe that they can close any deal. Even if that belief is true, which is seldom the case, it's not a good way to find either employers or clients for you or your services.

Most lawyers believe the broader their target market, the better opportunity there is for them to be retained. The same goes for lawyers seeking a new job. They believe they will find more job offers the more broadly they expand their search. Unfortunately for them, the opposite strategy is the most successful. Having a narrow target market is the most effective and efficient way to sell your services and find the perfect job.

When you're looking for the perfect job, if you try to be all things to all people, you can't present yourself as a top authority in any area. You can't distinguish yourself from the hordes of other lawyers with a broad target market. But, if you narrow your target market and focus on a particular industry, or even a segment of an industry, you can become an expert and distinguish yourself as a go-to person for the services you offer.

Whether you offer your services to an employer or a client, you need to know the most likely buyers. One of the best ways to consider your target market is to examine it from the perspective of the industries you will serve. While there are other ways lawyers decide on target markets, industry analysis is a good place to start.

The work you have done in identifying your purpose, passions, strengths, and interests, and in envisioning your ideal career, should help you narrow your target market. While narrow target markets are the best place to start, try not to rush to find your target market before you research potential target markets. Even if you are an experienced lawyer and you believe you know your target market well, now is the time to research to determine if there are other industries that need your services and solutions. Be inquisitive and open-minded. Identify the industries of employers or clients that need what you offer and will pay you to provide it. Some of the best opportunities to identify the perfect job happen during this research process.

Research on the internet. Brainstorm with trusted friends and colleagues. Use resources available from the professional organizations, your law school, and the government. One of the best ways to get perspective and advice in this target market exercise is to talk to legal career experts.

When considering a new job or career path, it's critical to have a clearly defined target market, for two reasons.

First, you can narrow your list of potential employers, whether you are interested in firms, corporations, or the government. Focus on organizations that serve your target market or which may want to expand to serve that target market.

Second, once you find a new job, you have a defined target market you can sell your services to at once. Even if you do not change jobs, identifying your target market can help you revitalize your career in your current position.

What is your target market?

LOCATION

When corporate turnaround professionals work with distressed businesses, they consider the location of the business's offices and other facilities. Important factors in the analysis include the ease of access for employees and clients, general amenities available in the area for employees and clients, and the proximity of the offices to clients and potential clients.

You should consider the same factors in revitalizing your distressed career. Research is important if you might need or want to move to a new section of the city, region, or country. Even if you are well-settled in your community and want to continue working and living in the same area, it's informative to spend a little time researching alternatives. You may confirm that the current locations of your office and home are fine. A few of you may decide you can satisfy more of your priorities by relocating your home or office, even if the move is just across town.

How easy is it for you to get to your office? How much time does it take? If your clients must visit your office, how convenient is it for them to do so?

For some lawyers, relocation of their office or home may improve their outlook on their career and life. The time spent and frustration caused by commuting can be an irritant, or worse. You may decide to move closer to your office to free up more time for activities outside the office with family or friends.

Relocating your home or office is much easier to do when you are younger, and before you have started a family. If you are younger, it's better to plan ahead than to believe you will always have the same mobility. For lawyers who already have families and roots in their communities, it may make sense to consider a change in the location of their office, which often means a change in employer. Even moving to a similar firm with similar compensation could be a wise career move if the time and hassle of your commute is reduced.

Does it make sense for you to consider a more drastic geographic relocation to another city or region of the country, or even the world? Will relocating help you find the perfect job and create your ideal career? Will you be able to go from your current job to the end of your ideal career in your present location? Does your current location give you the best opportunity to follow your ideal career path, or would your opportunities be better elsewhere?

Research can help you answer these questions if you are not already sure of the answers.

One consideration about your geographic location which is becoming more relevant is the possibility of working remotely. Many lawyers still believe that being in the same office as your colleagues is necessary for professional development and other purposes, but the strength of this belief has been lessening. More employers are permitting at least some remote work. Working remotely can free you from commuting and give you more flexibility in your schedule. Remote work doesn't fit everyone. If you are the type of person who likes to be around colleagues most of the time and finds being in the same office beneficial, remote work isn't a good choice for you.

Even further out on the spectrum of remote work is the concept of a virtual office. Law firms and other businesses are now being established with no, or few, physical offices. Everyone collaborates over the phone and digitally. This is an option to watch and even consider for those lawyers whose priorities include geographic mobility and work schedule flexibility. These arrangements may also be attractive on the back-end of your career as you cut back your work schedule and want more geographic flexibility in the location where you do your work.

A variation on the virtual firm is virtual temporary employment services. Instead of being a last resort for generating income, some lawyers prefer the temporary nature of the work and the geographic flexibility in their location that comes with that type of working arrangement. Those lawyers might consider companies like Axiom, one of the largest and fastest-growing businesses in the legal outsourcing and temping industry. Axiom's lawyers receive health insurance, paid time off, and 401(k) s. The lawyers' earnings are comparable to those of traditional firm or in-house lawyers. One of the biggest downsides of such employment arrangements is that work is not guaranteed, and when you are not working, you are not being paid.

Whether you are well-settled in your current home and office location or have unlimited flexibility to move anywhere in the world, consideration of your geographic location is important in any career revitalization process. Set aside some time to think through the issues and do any necessary research.

ORGANIZATIONS

You're clear on the perfect job and ideal career, but not on potential employers. You recognize the skills you wish to use in your next perfect job and your interests. You know the particular practice area or function where you will focus your job search efforts and the specific services you will offer to potential employers. You have decided on whether to offer your services to law firms, businesses, or the government. Focus the final stage of your research on specific organizations where you might want to work.

This discussion assumes you want to work in an organization. Some lawyers, even Big Law lawyers, may decide they want to work for themselves or create their own businesses. That's great! However, the research needed to make that career transition is much more involved. I recommend strongly that you work with a professional consultant, adviser or coach to consider what research you need to make that career transition.

Now, it's time to collect information on potential employers. You should have a good general idea of possible employers. But, you need to research on the internet, use your professional and personal networks, and use a direct contact strategy to learn more about potential employers. Don't just consider organizations with advertised job openings. Search for employers that might be a good fit for your skills and interests even if they have no listed job openings. What factors distinguish these potential employers? What makes them unique? What is their culture? Who are the power brokers? What are their biggest problems? What are their clients' most significant problems?

Learn about your potential employers. This information helps you decide which of them to focus on when conducting your job search campaign. The knowledge will also help you when you talk to these potential employers about possible positions where you can add value. The more information you have, the more discriminating you will be and the more prepared you are to convince potential employers why they should hire you.

There is a tremendous wealth of information available online. But, you will find the best information about potential employers by talking to other people. Use your networks. Contact people with information about potential employers you are researching. They might even work for the organizations on your list of potential employers.

You want to elicit the following information about potential employers:

- What's it like to work there?

- What's the culture?

- What is rewarded?

- What are the cardinal sins while working there?

- What problems is the employer facing?

- What problems are their clients facing?

- What is the biggest advantage of working there?

- What is the greatest headache in working there?

- Who are the power brokers?

- Who are the power brokers in the area you are interested in working?

- Is the employer growing, declining, or staying about the same size?

Make your own list of questions to add to the above list. Use the list as a guide when talking to people on the phone about potential employers. Know the questions well enough that you can recall the important areas you want to learn about when you meet people in person. Write down the answers to the questions. You believe you will remember the information you find, but you will only remember it if it's written. If you are meeting in person, carry a small notebook to take notes.

Patterns and typical answers should emerge about potential employers. Which organizations match your desires the closest? Keep honing in on those employers to discover your "A List" of potential employers that fit your criteria for an ideal employer.

CHAPTER 6
STRATEGIC PLANNING AND EXECUTION (PRIORITIES & ACTION)

Distressed businesses pay corporate turnaround professionals big dollars for strategic planning services. While many other functions are important to consider in revitalizing the company, strategic planning and implementation bring all the functions together.

Strategic planning and execution determine to a large degree whether a distressed company is restructured and revitalized, or whether the business fails. Some restructurings fail. When the preparatory work has been done thoroughly, though, and implementation actions consistently followed, the business has a good chance at being successfully revitalized.

Strategic planning and execution rest upon the preparatory analysis. If the company's purpose, passions, strengths, interests, and vision have not been thoroughly reviewed and aligned with the strategic plan, the plan will likely fail. It is only after all the preparatory work has been done that a successful strategic plan can be formulated and executed.

The same principles apply to your distressed career. Unless you have done the work in the earlier chapters, you will likely fall short of finding the perfect job and creating your ideal career. But, if you have done the preparatory work required, formulating a strategic plan and executing on that plan will lead to success, prosperity, and personal fulfillment in your career and life.

STRATEGIC PLAN

Pull up a chair. This is where your prior work pays off. This is the stage where your purpose, passions, strengths, interests, and vision come together in a strategic plan to find the perfect job and create your ideal career.

To formulate your strategic plan, start by identifying and marshaling your resources. Identify resources, including other people who can help you formulate and execute on your strategic plan.

Once you gather and identify all of your resources, you need the right mindset before you begin your strategic planning. A mindset where you are embracing creativity and possibilities. This mindset will take your strategic planning to a much higher level.

You have your resources. Your mindset is optimal. Now it's time to set priorities. You have needs and wants, financial constraints, and desires concerning the perfect job and ideal career. Despite some beliefs, you can't have it all. You will need to make hard choices and decide between attractive alternatives.

Once you decide on your priorities, you will be free to work on finding the perfect job and creating your ideal career.

The final stage of the strategic planning process is to be clear on your goals. Goals that are specific, measurable, achievable, realistic, and able to be accomplished within a set time.

Through the planning process, risk-adverse lawyers become more comfortable with ambiguity and the risks they perceive in their career paths. Plans are blueprints to guide your actions. Experience will deviate from the plan. That is no reason to throw away the plan. Instead, revisit the planning process to revise your plan in light of the new information.

While planning is important, it's not the plan that is most important; it's the planning process.

Again, for emphasis: planning is the key, not the plan.

IDENTIFY AND MARSHAL RESOURCES

Before you begin your planning, identify and marshal your resources. You have already done most of the work by getting clear on the requirements for the perfect job and ideal career. Now, you need to focus on and organize resources to achieve your goals.

Organize your resources in these categories:

TIME

How much time do you have to work on your career revitalization? Silly question, right? If you are working, you don't believe you have any time. If you are not working, you may feel you have unlimited time. Both beliefs are wrong.

If you are working but are not satisfied with your job or career path, you must make time for this process. How much time depends on how much pain or fear you are experiencing and how motivated you are to find you perfect job and create your ideal career. You are reading this book. That's a good start, but many people read lots of career books and then do nothing. They are wasting their time if they are not taking action.

Commit to working on your career revitalization for a fixed number of hours each week. Schedule the tasks in your calendar; don't just put them on your to-do list. Treat the scheduled career time as a top priority, just like client work. Protect that time and, if you must reschedule due to unanticipated events, reschedule the time during the same week. Even if you work late or come in early to do it. Unless you treat your career time as sacrosanct, it will end up as one of those items on your calendar and to-do list that keeps being carried, but never being accomplished.

How much time should you devote to your career revitalization? How badly do you want to find the perfect job? How quickly do you want to create your ideal career path to success, prosperity, and personal fulfillment?

I urge you to devote at least five hours per week to this process, even if you are not facing any immediate fear or pain concerning your job. If you are in a more intense situation, fifteen hours per week is a good benchmark. And if you are not working, forty hours per week should be the minimum. It will be difficult to reach these targets. You will most likely need to schedule time on the weekends, early mornings, or late evenings. If you are not working, forty hours may seem like a breeze if you were billing fifty or sixty hours per week when you were working. But, you continue to have other obligations. You may also pick up more household and childcare duties. Diversions magically appear. There are no real deadlines unless your financial situation is precarious. It's easy to get to the end of the week and realize you haven't worked on your career revitalization for your scheduled time commitment.

FINANCIAL

What are your financial resources?

If you are not working, how long until you need an income-producing job?

How much can you spend on career-related information and professional help? Do you have the financial resources to buy various professional assessments or subscribe to data resources? Can you find the money to hire professional consultants, advisers, or coaches?

There are trade-offs. You may spend a little less time on the career revitalization process if you have the funds to hire professionals. These professionals can assist you in being more efficient and focused in you work, and may even do some of the work for you. If your funds are limited, and you can't afford outside help, you may need to spend more time on career matters.

FAMILY, FRIENDS, AND COLLEAGUES

Do you have family, friends, or colleagues who can help with you career revitalization? These are people who can help in ways beyond networking. These individuals must have both the time and the skills to be a useful resource. Otherwise, they will just divert you from your primary focus.

When using family, friends, or colleagues as career revitalization resources, you need to be careful. These individuals need clear roles. Their desire to be helpful when they don't possess the knowledge or the skills to do so, and the potential for emotions influencing judgments, are possible issues. Family members may be affected by issues about money. Colleagues may be influenced by a desire to continue working with you. You also need to be cautious when letting colleagues into your career revitalization process if you don't want your current employer to know about your plans.

What resources will you use in your career revitalization process?

SET PRIORITIES

Your success, prosperity, and personal fulfillment are determined by how closely your career and life are in alignment with your purpose, passions, interests, and vision.

In your career, you may strive for mastery, status, power, and high income. In your personal life, you may want close relationships, family time, and the freedom to pursue hobbies and other non-work-related activities.

In setting career goals and making plans to achieve these objectives, you need to consider not only your career, but also the other areas of your life. While the holy grail for many lawyers is a work-life balance, this is seldom accomplished without carefully prioritizing career and life goals.

Trade-offs are required. The balance in one person's life may look much different from the balance in someone else's life. The key is to make informed, intentional decisions on the trade-offs that are right for your life and vision.

We all know lawyers who appear successful by any measure, but we learn they are unfulfilled and miserable. Why? One reason may be because the trade-offs they made between their work and personal life resulted in a failure to focus on any goals other than their career goals.

A recent study of over 6,000 lawyers published in the George Washington Law Review found that the strongest predictors of lawyers' well-being were autonomy, relatedness to others, feelings of competence, and choosing work for internally motivated reasons. The study notes:

These data consistently indicate that a happy life as a lawyer is much less about grades, affluence, and prestige than about finding work that is interesting, engaging, personally meaningful, and focused on providing needed help to others.

"What Makes Lawyers Happy?: A Data Driven Prescription to Redefine Professional Success" (Vol. 83, No. 2, Feb. 2015).

One of the most startling findings in the study is that money had a negative correlation with happiness among the respondents.

We all dream of our ideal careers and life. Most of us have our "champagne wishes and caviar dreams." I hope your career visioning process resulted in many specific and detailed goals.

Now it's time to stop dreaming, and start prioritizing your goals. No matter how much we dream or desire, we can't have it all. Choose those goals that are most important to you, and focus your action and energy on those goals to find the perfect job and create your ideal career.

NEEDS/WANTS

Needs are something essential and necessary to sustain your existence. Wants are a feeling for something you believe you lack.

In prioritizing your goals, focus on your needs first and then your wants. Prioritizing is a subjective process for every lawyer, and there will be significant interrelationships between your needs and wants. The tricky part is differentiating between your needs and wants.

For some lawyers, an income of $60,000 satisfies their needs (although they may want much more), while others insist that they need an income exceeding $600,000 to meet their needs. Since your expenditures are a proxy for a bundle of many of your needs and wants, it is helpful to break those needs and wants down by creating a budget.

It is often useful to start your prioritization process by using your budget to consider the items that are needs and those that are wants. After considering financial matters, you will want to look at your needs and wants in relation to your work environment and colleagues. You will also need to prioritize your needs and wants in relation to your family, relationships, community activity, and personal time.

These sections focus on different areas where you will prioritize your needs and wants.

FINANCIAL REQUIREMENTS

None of us would refuse a little (or a lot) more income. We could always use the excess to satisfy our unsatisfied wants and desires. If our needs and most of our wants are satisfied, spending the extra income on others or donating it to worthy causes would make most of us happy.

There is a minimum level of income which we all need to survive and live a reasonable lifestyle. There are many variables in ascertaining the amount necessary for each of us. Factors such as our spouse's income, our wealth, our debts, our lifestyle, the number of children we have, and where we live all affect the income necessary to meet our needs.

We all need a place to live. For some, a basic apartment or house will be okay. For others, they believe they would be miserable without a large house in the best part of town. What accounts for the difference? Not needs, but wants and desires.

Once your basic need is satisfied, individual desires are the pre-dominant factor. These desires spring from our backgrounds, our aspirations, and our relative positions compared to our family and friends. Our families can also influence our desires.

The same analysis applies to other categories of expenditures and investments, from food to recreation to travel to savings. You have needs and wants. Since you don't have unlimited financial resources, you allocate those resources to cover all of your needs first. Then, you allocate the remaining funds to your wants in a way that provides maximum satisfaction. Preparing a budget is a priority-setting process.

Once your basic needs are satisfied, consider the following: do you eat out every night, take expensive vacations, send your kids to private schools, or increase your savings and investments? Your choices are your priorities. What are your priorities?

Schedule a time on your calendar to consider your finances and sketch out a rough budget at your current income level. How do you allocate your funds? What are your basic needs? What are your most desired wants?

The budgeting process helps you think about your priorities in a concrete way. Are there different allocations of your income that could produce greater overall happiness? Are what you've thought of as needs really wants instead? Is there a way to reduce your expenditures in certain areas while maintaining your current level of satisfaction?

There are several caveats to note when using a budget to help clarify your priorities. Scientific studies find we overestimate the satisfaction we will receive from satisfying our wants. We may believe with all our heart that the big house on the hill will complete our life and produce never-ending ecstasy. That may be the result for a few weeks, months, or years. But much sooner than you might think, the glow wears off. The reality sets in, and you realize your satisfaction level has decreased. This occurs because you desire an even bigger and more ornate house, or because you realize there are fewer funds to spend or invest in other areas.

A second caveat is the principle of diminishing marginal returns in relation to your spending. While eating at the finest restaurants is a great treat and can add significant levels of satisfaction to some lawyers' lives, doing it five nights a week is less appealing. At that point, an occasional plain spinach salad or greasy burger provides a far greater amount of satisfaction.

The moral is to be careful when considering your needs and wants, and in attributing various levels of satisfaction to spending funds in a particular area. Some people may derive a continuing high level of satisfaction from having the big house; others are more satisfied by allocating funds to exotic vacations or putting money in the bank for education or retirement.

WORK ENVIRONMENT

Many lawyers spend well over a third of their lives working. The environment you work in is an important determinant of your success, prosperity, and personal fulfillment. Your choices concerning your work environment reflect your priorities. Sometimes a change in your work environment, without a change in your job, can make a huge difference in your career and life.

Unfortunately, our jobs are a package deal. While we may find a few add-on features or a little personalization in some instances, the package deal is standard. In the career revitalization process, a broad view is required in order to analyze all of your priorities in your work environment.

The organization you work for, its size, the working conditions and amenities, your colleagues, your role, and the geographic location of your office are the main factors comprising your work environment.

TYPE OF ORGANIZATION

What kind of organization do you want to work in?

You can work for a for-profit organization, a not-for-profit organization, a governmental organization, or yourself. The organization can be well-established or a start-up. Each type of organization has a different work environment. Each organization within each category has its own work environment. Even each office within an organization has a somewhat unique environment.

When considering the perfect job, what are your most important priorities? If money is a top priority, you will gravitate to Big Law. If social justice is a top priority, you will move toward smaller firms, legal aid organizations, or the government. The choice of an organization comes as a package. You are unlikely to have a big office overlooking the city when working for legal aid organizations. Your ability to be heavily involved in social justice is likely limited in Big Law. There are trade-offs involved in each decision, and à la carte menus are seldom an option.

Be clear on your priorities. It is critical to being successful, prosperous, and personally fulfilled in your career and life. If your priorities are to work with start-up entrepreneurs and be involved with business as well as legal issues, a Big Law job may not be your best choice. Or, it may be. If your immediate priorities are to pay down your student debt and get a few years of experience, Big Law may be a great option, even if you won't immediately be doing the work you desire in your ideal career.

When considering your priorities, what type of organization is most attractive? Will your answer be different depending on the time frame?

SIZE OF ORGANIZATION

What size organization do you want to work in? Do you want to be a solo practitioner or entrepreneur, or work in a global Am Law 100 firm or Fortune 100 company?

Think about the size of the organization which is right for you and your priorities. Do you want more freedom and flexibility, as found in a smaller organization, or more resources and varied opportunities that might be found in larger organizations?

Also consider the size of the local office within the organization. Size is important when you consider larger organizations. Would the local office of the organization be the home office or a satellite office? Would it be a small office within a large organization, or a larger office within a smaller organization?

The answers to these questions can be significant when considering your priorities. Consider the trade-offs. There may be ways to balance your desires with organization size. If you want the feel of a smaller organization, but also want the resources of a larger organization, a smaller office in a large organization might fit. There are other considerations even within a balance like this. Smaller offices within larger organizations, including law firms, generally have fewer opportunities for advancement.

What size organization and what size office is the best fit for your priorities?

WORKING CONDITIONS AND AMENITIES

You may not have much control over your physical working conditions. Many employers have existing locations with fixed office layouts and they assign working spaces according to seniority or some other factor. In many offices, the furniture is standard issue and may even be fixed in place. Some employers limit the amount of personalization allowed on the walls and credenzas.

If your physical working conditions are important, remember this when considering potential employers. The physical working conditions and the flexibility allowed for personalization can be different among similar employers. When accepting an offer for a job, remember that your negotiating leverage is always higher before you take the position. If your physical working space is important, negotiate the best deal you can in regard to those items up front.

Office amenities are not a high priority for most lawyers, but they are a factor that should be considered in the total mix of the perfect job and ideal career.

Office amenities, particularly at the high-end, may also intersect with income considerations. Complimentary access to child care services, top health clubs, breakfast and lunch facilities or clubs, dry-cleaning services, and access to a concierge are offered by some employers. The downside of cushy perks is usually a culture where long hours in the office are expected. Trade-offs are a reality.

If these amenities and services are something you would purchase anyway, include the cost when comparing different compensation packages.

COLLEAGUES

What type of colleagues do you want to work with? Do you want to work alone? Do you crave friendly colleagues who relate to each other in a loose manner? Or, do you prefer to work with the top experts in your field no matter what their personalities or the nature of the working relationship? When lawyers' preferences toward their colleagues are not aligned with the environment of their office, the disconnect can lead to significant dissatisfaction with their work.

Collegiality is a factor which is hard to judge before accepting a job offer. When talking to potential employers or interviewing with them, they are on their best behavior. Everyone is friendly and welcoming. The interviews are held on a different floor than that of the yellers and screamers.

One clue to assessing your potential colleagues at a particular employer is to look at the background of the people working there. Did they graduate from the same schools, do they belong to the same associations, or were they raised in the same area of the country? The background of your potential colleagues is relevant information. Especially if you didn't go to those schools, belong to those associations, or were raised in a different part of the country or world. Lack of diversity of all kinds may be a decisive factor for some lawyers. Especially if you are outside of the norm for that employer.

The more people you talk with who either work with the employer, or have worked or dealt with the employer in another capacity, the better. Even in the most guarded of environments, at some point you will likely find little hints of the real atmosphere, or at least develop a gut feeling.

You need to get clarity on the culture and office atmosphere, and be honest with yourself before you accept a job. Many lawyers can be seduced by money or other factors and rationalize they can deal with any culture or office atmosphere. Most of the time, their rationalizations turn into dissatisfaction or worse, and money doesn't relieve the pain.

YOUR ROLE

When you accept a position, the position dictates your role. Be sure of the expectations up front. Are you expected to be a manager, supervisor, or leader? Will you need to devote time to office administration or committee work? Will you need to be involved with recruiting or general office business development efforts? Will you have the opportunity or obligation, depending on how you view it, to participate in managing the employer? Will you be expected to attend many functions or outings?

All of these potential obligations require your time and effort. You may enjoy some and detest others. It is best to know before committing to an employer their expectations of your role outside of your work, so know this before you commit. Otherwise, you may be unpleasantly surprised.

Be clear on what you want your role to be with an employer. Do you want to work alone or as part of a team? Do you want responsibilities outside of your core job functions? Do you want to be involved with the administration or management of the employer? These are all questions you should decide on and prioritize before you formulate your action plan.

GEOGRAPHIC LOCATION

The first question to ask yourself regarding location is where you want to work. For some lawyers, it seems almost self-evident. They grew up or went to school in a particular area, and they don't want to leave. Others may gravitate to the largest city in the region with the most opportunities. For a smaller group of lawyers, national or even international geographic mobility is the norm.

I have lived and worked in seven cities across the United States, and moved at least twice that number of times in my career. I will move at least twice more. While I am flexible and look forward to working and living in different locations, relocation is difficult.

Think about geographic location long and hard, and early in your career. Consider the long-term arc of your career and your current preferences. Analyze the potential opportunities to create your ideal career over the long-term, not just in relation to your next perfect job.

The decision on your location may limit possible alternatives in other areas. If you want to live and work in Steamboat Springs, Colorado, you will not work at an Am Law 100 firm. If you wish to live in various places and travel, you need to consider becoming a solo entrepreneur with a digital platform. Or, work with an organization that has a virtual business model.

Many lawyers work in the same geographic location for their entire career. Preference accounts for some of this tendency, but state bar licensing requirements also restrict the geographical mobility of lawyers. I was an unusual case; I practiced law and am licensed in three jurisdictions – the District of Columbia, New York, and Alabama. I waived into the DC Bar, but took the bar examinations in both New York and Alabama. I was also an in-house counsel in Florida, although geographical constraints on in-house counsel are much less restrictive.

Geographic restrictions apply to lawyers who actively practice law, and are slowly breaking down. I suspect there will be a form of national licensing within the next ten years. With the reciprocity accommodations of many state bar associations and the likely advent of a national bar examination, restrictions on lawyer mobility will ease. While California and Florida – states that are attractive semi-retirement work locations – may hold out, restrictions on lawyers' geographic mobility are easing.

When considering your geographic location, keep the future in mind. Will you need the flexibility to move to a different area in the future? What are your spouse's thoughts about geographic location, now and in the future?

The final consideration relating to geographic priorities is the actual location of where you live and work within a particular geographic area. Do you want to work in the central business district or in the suburbs? Do you want to live in the central business district or in the suburbs? It is easier to move within a particular area than to move to a different city or region of the country, but it can still be a pain.

One of the biggest factors in choosing where you work and where you live is the commuting time. Some lawyers may want the freedom of a small office close to where they live. They may desire to work from home at least part-time, or to work while traveling. If you have leverage (read: a book of business), these arrangements may be negotiable.

Even if you can arrange for your work location to deviate from the norm of your employer, consider the potential ramifications. Sometimes, even if you have the freedom to work remotely, as a practical matter, your job requires you to be in the employer's offices most of the time. In addition, the lack of actual face-time with your colleagues may adversely affect your opportunities for advancement.

There is even a small subset of lawyers where their physical work location outside of a traditional office is a top priority. If this is your top priority, trying to negotiate a compromised arrangement with a traditional legal employer will not satisfy you. Instead, you may be more suited to a solo practice. Or, working with one of the New Law organizations with business models based on virtual offices or other alternative office arrangements.

DECISION TIME

Okay, time to decide. It's nice to have plenty of options, but a strategic plan must be detailed and focused on one option in each area. It's fine to have alternative strategies and back-up plans, but that is for when you reach insurmountable road-blocks in implementing your strategic plan. For now, only one choice in each area is allowed.

Once you have researched different jobs and careers, con-sidered your options and priorities, it is time to decide. **Make a decision for each category and rank the categories against each other according to your priorities.**

This exercise gives you an outline for your strategic plan to find the perfect job, create your ideal career, and achieve suc-cess, prosperity, and personal fulfillment.

- **Type -** Firm, In-House, Government, Non-Legal, or Entrepre-neurial

- **Size -** Big Law, Regional, Specialty, Local, or Boutique

- **Working Conditions And Amenities** - Specify

- **Colleagues** - Specify

- **Role -** Specify

- **Location** - Specify

Once you rank the major factors of the perfect job and ideal career, you need to fill in the information from your research regarding different organizations or opportunities that may be available for the perfect job and ideal career.

The next step is to go back over your strategic plan and set goals related to your top priorities.

GOALS

Once you have the framework of your strategic plan in place, it's time to set goals. Goals allow you to formulate action plans, and take the steps to find the perfect job and create your ideal career. After you create a strategic plan, you are ready to set goals and make plans to reach your objectives.

Goal setting is a multifaceted process. Your highest level goal is to realize your vision of an ideal career and life. That is too broad and not useful in your knowing the actions to take to make it happen. Your next level goal is to find the perfect job. Great, but there are many levels of goals below that before you find the perfect job. The goal setting aspect of comprehensive strategic planning is about breaking down each successive goal until you get to the specific goals you can achieve within a short time. Although you can't work directly on the top level goal of realizing your ideal career, this goal setting process will yield quite a few goals you can work on immediately.

You need to write down your work in the goal setting process. Work backward from your ideal career until you have goals you can take action on now and achieve within a short time. These goals will serve as the basis for your action plan and immediate day-to-day activities.

SMART GOALS

The best goal setting process I have found requires you to decide on specific, measurable, attainable, and relevant goals you can achieve within a set time. This process is the SMART Goal setting process. It's an excellent framework in goal setting work.

Your goals should be specific. Such as, "I will make networking calls on Wednesday afternoon to reconnect with colleagues at a prior job and get an update on they are doing now." Not, "I will do some networking this week."

The goals must be measurable. Such as, "I will make at least five calls this week." Not, "I will make some networking calls."

The goals should be attainable. Such as, "I will talk to at least three people this week." Not, "I will speak to all twenty people in my old department this week."

The goals must be relevant. Such as, "I will make these networking calls because I can share useful information with these individuals, and they may be in a position to help me later." Not, "I want to find out how the old softball team is doing this year."

The goals should be time bound. Such as, "I will make these calls from 3:00 to 4:00 on Wednesday afternoon." Not, "I will make these calls when I'm free for a few minutes."

You identify goals which you need to achieve in order to move forward, and to find the perfect job and create your ideal career. These objectives will have different time horizons to finish, and will relate to many areas in your career and life.

Break your goals down into short-term goals you can achieve within the next ninety days, intermediate-term goals you can achieve within ninety and one-hundred and eighty days, and long-term goals you cannot achieve within one-hundred eighty days.

After you decide on and set specific, measurable, attainable, and relevant goals you can complete by a particular date, it is time to take consistent action to move you forward along your ideal career path.

ACTION PLAN

We now turn our attention to executing on your strategic plan. Your plan to identify and find the perfect job and create your ideal career. You've formulated your strategic plan with your priorities incorporated and set your short-term, intermediate-term, and long-term goals. You know where you want to go. Now, how do you get there?

You implement your strategic plan and achieve the associated goals by creating an action plan. An action plan includes all activities required for you to attain your goals. It is like a comprehensive to-do list. But what sets the career revitalization action plan apart from traditional to-do lists is that all action plan tasks must be scheduled on your calendar.

Your do-list gets those action items out of your head in order to free up your brain circuits for more important work than using them as a file cabinet. But, until the tasks are on your calendar, they don't lead to action. To-do lists can give rise to the opposite of action, procrastination, and overwhelm you when you see how many tasks you want to accomplish.

You use your worksheets from the goal setting section to specify tasks to put on your action list. Take every short-term goal on the goal list and write every step you must take to accomplish that goal. Make a notation of whether you can take the action immediately, or whether that action depends on you having taken prior action.

Consider all the action items you can act on now. It is best to write them on a separate sheet of paper. Examine those action items and determine which of them is most important for you to accomplish today, this week, and this month. Estimate the time it will take to complete each task. You will underestimate the time a task will take, sometimes by as much as half. Be realistic and give yourself a cushion in making estimates of the time required to complete each task. When you put the action items on your calendar, it is much better to finish early than to not be able to finish. If you don't complete a task in the allotted time, it will create stress. Stress caused by not finishing the task, or because it compromises your time on some other matter on your schedule.

You are ready to take your action list and schedule the tasks on your calendar. Start with a calendar that has all of your pre-existing commitments. Schedule any other work or family time you need. "Okay", I can hear you screaming, "I don't have time for my existing commitments, much less any new career revitalization tasks." Agreed, you don't have the time if you want to continue to be disengaged from your work and dissatisfied with your life. Go ahead and say you don't have time. I stayed in jobs that were not perfect, and on career paths that were not ideal, for years. No, decades. What an unnecessary waste. You career and life will not get better until you take the time to do the tasks required to find the perfect job and create your ideal career.

You need to find the time. You need to cut back on non-essential items. No more Facebook or Twitter. No more television. Shorter lunches and dinners. Less time with colleagues and friends unless you can accomplish one of your career revitalization tasks while you are with them. Don't cut back on your sleep or fitness activities. Try to increase both if you've been neglecting them. Sleep and fitness will give you more energy to work effectively and efficiently.

JOB SEARCH

This section covers material that comprises the bulk of many job search books. It is the nuts and bolts of the job search process. If you haven't completed the prior sections, taking the actions here will be nowhere near as effective. Although you may find some helpful tips, your career revitalization will suffer without first taking the steps suggested in earlier chapters. Even if you don't have a good grasp of who you are and where you want to go, this section can help you find a job. But, it will not be the perfect job or the job that puts you on your ideal career path.

You will use the skills you developed as a lawyer in this part of your career revitalization process. Your research and investigation skills will help you uncover jobs and opportunities. When interviewing, or even discussing potential employment, act as if you are working on a litigation file or doing due diligence. Your mission is to uncover the most relevant information about the employer and its employees. The essential information you need to propose a solution to the issues and problems which the employer and its clients are facing. You also need to focus on information about the key items on your priority list, and how well the position and organization fit your vision of the perfect job.

JOB SEARCH PROCESS

To find a job, solve a problem of an employer. Convince the employer you can solve their problem. You need to persuade them you are the best person for the job.

You will act as a consultant. You need to collect information and listen to what you are told about the employer's needs and problems. You must ask questions designed to elicit information to help you formulate a solution. The solution includes you as a new employee.

It is a mistake to sell your education, experience, and other qualifications in the abstract. You must discover what problems the employer has that keep them awake at night. At a later stage, even after an interview, you show the employer how you can help them solve their problems and sleep better. This is the same process top rainmakers use to attract clients, and which Apple uses to sell its products. Don't sell your skills and awesomeness – instead, sell the solution to the employer's problems.

This same process can be used internally if you are employed, but not in the perfect job. If you like your employer, but not your job, the easiest way to find the perfect job is to follow this process with your current employer. First, do your research to discover problems and formulate solutions. Then, propose creating a position with your employer which you will fill. Search for problems your organization has not solved. If you have the passion, interest, and skills to solve those problems, pursue it. If a possible path to the perfect job and ideal career can be crafted at your current employer, it minimizes the inevitable disruptions that occur when you change employers. This strategy has much to recommend it.

If you don't have the perfect job, and can't figure out how to create the perfect job with your current employer, it is time to look elsewhere. Your first action shouldn't be clicking on lawyer job search sites or calling a headhunter. Your first action should be to pull out your workbooks with your strategic plan, goal list, and action plan. Then, schedule the action item tasks on your calendar and complete the tasks. You know what you need to do to find to where you want to go. All that's lacking is action.

Some of you may reply, "Yes, but I checked, and there are no available jobs at any of the employers on my ideal employer target list." Wonderful! You won't need to fight the crowd of applicants for every position advertised. You have an open path to discover the employer's problems and then offer yourself as the savior with the solution. This is the best way for a lawyer to find a new job. You create the job, and write the job description and employment contract yourself. As long as you convince the employer you can solve one of their significant problems, there will be a job created just for you.

What if you notice a job opening at an employer you are interested in? Go for it. But realize that the employer may not even know their problem. Even if they are advertising for a job opening. A typical situation where this occurs is when an employee leaves. The employer may put up the same job description it originally used to hire the employee who has left. Even if the job description was accurate when first used, the problems the employer or its clients were focused on at the time might have changed. Or, the job description may not have been accurate the first time.

It is much easier for an employer to specify qualifications and job responsibilities than to describe a problem they are trying to solve. This is why most jobs are advertised with qualifications and responsibilities. It is easier to screen lawyers out if there are quantifiable hurdles to being granted an interview. Even the people doing the interviewing may not know, or may not volunteer, the problem they are hoping to solve with their new hire. That is why it is so important for you to research, listen closely, and ask questions. Even if you don't have the advertised qualifications or experience, you can pinpoint the problems and offer solutions. This will give you a better chance of being offered the job.

REENTERING THE JOB MARKET

Did you leave your job as a lawyer a few (or more) years ago? Perhaps you took a sabbatical to raise your kids, to pursue a start-up dream, or as the result of the "Great Recession" which started in 2008.

Now you're considering jumping back into the shark-filled waters of the legal industry (are you sure?). If you're a lawyer who has been out of the legal industry for an extended period, what do you do first? How should you approach your job search?

There is no difference in how you approach your job search, whether you've been out of the legal industry for an extended period or not. You conduct your job search as consultants approach their work.

Do focused research on the status of the legal industry, practice area, and firms or other employers where you might be interested in working. Determine the problems that your targeted firms and their clients confront. Create a storyline detailing how you can use your skills and experience to solve those problems. Spotlight skills and experience acquired while working as a lawyer as well as outside of the legal industry. You also need to reestablish a personal brand, combining your expertise and personal traits to bolster your job search.

It is important not to overestimate the weight which employers give to your prior experience. Realize how fast the legal industry is evolving. Law firms and other potential employers are reluctant to hire lawyers who haven't practiced for a while. Firms assume you are not up to date on problems in the legal field and your practice area. They think that your contacts aren't fresh and your skills are not sharp.

You address these employer concerns by doing your homework and researching what is going on in your field. Reestablish connections with contacts you let go stale. Prove your skills are sharp by finding a relevant short-term freelance or volunteer position to get references supporting your current skills. Take short refresher courses or get certifications if appropriate for your practice area.

You will find a job and make a career comeback. You will do it with style and grace. It will be a job where you will be successful, prosperous, and personally fulfilled. The key to finding the perfect job is determining how you can help potential employers and their clients solve their problems. Once you do that, law firms and other organizations will be out-bidding each other for your services.

When your job search process succeeds, and you reenter the legal industry, then what? Expect to be shocked that you are not up to speed in a particular field or with specific skills. This will be true, no matter how much you research and prepare. The time and energy you will need to feel comfortable in your new position will be much greater than you imagine. Technology is integrating itself into more areas of the practice of law. Get comfortable using the new technology in your work quickly.

Some colleagues and support staff will be skeptical of your abilities and capabilities. Expect it. You will prove yourself over time and win them over.

When you're a lawyer who's been out of the legal industry for a significant time, it's hard to reenter the industry. However, if you do your research, identify employer problems, and craft a story showing how you can solve those problems, you will find the perfect job.

RESUME

Resumes are still a necessary evil when searching for a job. When applying for advertised jobs, know that there are ways to increase the odds of passing a machine scan. If you follow the advice in this section, you will optimize your resume for both machines and humans.

If you want your resume to be seen by humans and to lead to an interview, it should be:

1. Clear, well-organized, and concise.

2. Customized for each position.

3. Tailored with keywords used in the advertisement or listing, especially those in qualifications and job descriptions.

4. Focused on the employer's needs, not on your experience and education.

5. Filled with quantifiable achievements related to items in the job description.

6. Honest and accurate, but don't be afraid to tout your accomplishments and showcase them in the best light.

If you follow these six principles, your resume will be better than 95% of all resumes. Your resume will stand out, and it will pass through machine scanning programs and be considered by people reviewing the most qualified candidates.

Use a current format for your resume. Not the same form you used ten years ago when you did your last job search. As long as you use a current format with a classic look (you appreciate that the legal industry is still traditional and conservative), your resume will be fine.

The most important thing about a resume is that it focuses on the specific employer and the particular job. Each resume you send should be customized. It is a lot of work, but well worth it.

I don't recommend mass-mailing resumes. I don't recommend sending a resume in response to every new opening. And, I don't recommend having a form resume posted on any website, whether it is your site or a commercial job site.

The chances of getting an interview, much less a job, from a blind resume, are almost nil. Spend your time on customizing resumes for positions that would be the perfect job for you. Tailor the resume so it creates a story of why you are the best person to fill the opening.

A targeted rifle approach, not a scatter-shot shotgun approach, is how to go with resumes.

Anyone who wants to check your professional qualifications will use LinkedIn. Customize your resume so it is optimized to appeal to an employer with the perfect job and modify each time you send it out. Only use a resume when required, and make sure it follows the six principles listed above.

LINKEDIN

LinkedIn is the gold standard of professional job and career sites. It was built as a professional job and networking site. Today, LinkedIn has many features you can use in your career revitalization process.

Your online efforts should start with crafting a complete and optimized LinkedIn profile. You must upload your picture, this being a professional picture and not a selfie. A LinkedIn profile without a professional headshot has no credibility. If you don't have a professional headshot, get one. Or, find a family member or friend who knows something about photography to take your headshot with you in business attire.

Your professional headline is the text that appears under your name on your LinkedIn profile. By default, your current job title will appear. Edit the professional headline by deleting your job title and replacing it with a short statement directed at your target audience. Your ideal employers and clients are your top two target audiences. Make your professional headline a clear statement of who you serve and what problems you solve.

Your professional headline must speak to the solution for a primary problem of your target audience. If you are looking for a job, make your professional headline a short job description highlighting who you serve. Don't put "Corporate attorney" – put "Mid-level Big Law attorney helping software startups negotiate first round venture capital deals." Instead of "Real estate attorney," your professional headline might read: "Attorney assisting developers to get zoning approval for their commercial real estate projects in northern New Jersey." Or, "Lawyer helping financial service companies enforce their default remedies against hotel borrowers nationwide."

You want one or two words indicating the function you perform. For lawyers, it will be "lawyer" or "attorney." There is no reason to specify the type of lawyer since the rest of your professional headline shows what you do. The key to the remainder of the headline is to use keywords to show the type of client you serve and the problem you solve. If your services are limited to a particular geographic area, this should also be included.

Tailor your prior job descriptions to focus on the problems you solved and the results you achieved. The more quantifiable results you can showcase, the better. Results are significant credibility builders. Remember, the job description is not about what you did or the functions you performed – it is about concrete outcomes and results.

JOB SEARCHES ON LINKEDIN

To start your job search on LinkedIn, click on the "Jobs" tab under the search bar on your homepage. The page that opens has a "Jobs" search box at the top of the page.

However, before you search, look at the section below the search box. This section is labeled "Jobs you may be interested in" and lists jobs selected for you by LinkedIn based on your profile. You can refine the LinkedIn selections by specifying a preferred geographic location, company size, and industry.

Below "Jobs you may be interested in" is a "Discover jobs in your network" section. This section has information on job listings with companies where you are already connected to someone on LinkedIn – another reason to build your LinkedIn network. The information shown includes the number of people you have relationships with at that firm or company and the number of job listings. These job listings shown are for all jobs, not just lawyer jobs. If you click on the employer, it will take you to their LinkedIn page with the job listings.

Then go back up to the top of the Jobs page. Click on the "Advanced search" button and then the "More options" button. This will take you to the Advanced Search page. Type in your search keywords and specify your search filters to find the jobs on LinkedIn that fit the criteria of the perfect job. You can search and filter the results by keywords, company name, job title, location, country, zip code, date posted, industry, experience level, and job function. You need a premium account to filter by salary.

Recent searches on the LinkedIn site returned 5,443 jobs for the term "lawyer" and 7,901 jobs for the term "attorney."

Don't waste your time on other sites; go straight to LinkedIn to look for jobs as a lawyer. If you want to browse other job search sites, read the section on job search sites in the Appendix.

I described the tip of the LinkedIn job search iceberg. There are other great features in the "Jobs" section to help lawyers find job listings. You can also use LinkedIn in other ways to assist in your job search and the career revitalization process. It is an excellent tool for research, networking, self-promotion, and getting referrals.

NETWORKING

You can't successfully revitalize your distressed legal career by yourself. You can't find the perfect job by yourself. You need other people to assist you. Your networks of personal and professional contacts can provide information, assistance, advice, and access to other people and resources. Members of your networks might provide leads to help you find the perfect job.

You must take consistent action to establish, maintain, and nurture your personal and professional networks. The contacts in your networks will be an excellent resource to use in meeting and connecting with other people in a position to help you.

The most important thing to remember about any active network of contacts is that the relationships are mutual. You must assist others and provide value to them before you can expect that they will help you. That is why consistent focus on maintaining and nurturing the contacts in your networks is essential.

Networking is a key aspect of finding the perfect job.

Networking is covered in detail in the Marketing And Sales Chapter.

INTERVIEWING

"Once you get an interview, the race is won. Right?" No, you are still closer to the starting line than the finish line.

You want to take all the actions recommended by interviewing experts. Dress in clean business clothes, arrive at the interview a few minutes early, take copies of your resume, smile a lot, and be pleasant. Great stuff. But, these actions are expected. What will set you apart from the other candidates?

The best advice. Do your background research on the employer and anyone else you are likely to meet. Act like a consultant during your interviews. Listen. Ask questions designed to find information about the problems that must be solved. Probe behind the stock responses and uncover what is driving the need for a new employee. Find out what the perfect candidate would look like to the employer.

Script out the questions you want to ask and the points you want to make beforehand. Ask pertinent and penetrating questions designed to find out what problems the employer and its clients face. Questions about what keeps them up at night. Questions that let your interviewers know you are prepared and that you think like a problem solver. This is not something most employers see often in an interview and it will set you apart from the other candidates for the job.

Take notes during the interview, or if not during the interview, right after the interview. If taking notes in the interview, use pen and paper, not a computer or other electronic device. Using electronic devices in interviews can be very distracting to the interviewer and may be seen as a disrespectful practice.

The real work comes after the interview. Examine your notes. Brainstorm potential solutions to the problems you identified. Think about what you heard. Do more research. Make a few calls to bounce ideas off of other people. Then outline a plan to solve the employer's problems. Put it into letter format and deliver it to everyone in the hiring chain.

Sit back and wait for the offer to be extended.

SALARY

Negotiations about salary are best left to the end of the process. Many employers will try to get a number from you, but resist any urge to throw one out. Tell them it is unrealistic for you to give them a compensation number before you discuss the nature of the job and the exact expectations. Or before they hear how much value you will add to their organization. Focus on adding value and helping the employer in ways they might not yet imagine. If the employer continues to force a number, or will not go further without you throwing a number out, ask them for the number they will willingly pay the successful candidate. Tell them you will then either go forward or thank them for their time.

If you must put a number on the table, give them a number at the high end of your range, with 10% added on to your high number. Don't back down when they react with feigned shock.

Just tell them you think you can add much more value to the employer, but that until there are further discussions, you are not prepared to negotiate a number. Let them know that, if an offer is extended, you will be happy to work with them to figure out a fair compensation for your services. Make them aware you want to be on their side of the table. That you will work with them on compensation which is fair to everyone, based on the value you will bring to the organization. When you convince the employer you can solve their problems and add value, you shouldn't have trouble agreeing on a fair compensation package.

When negotiating a compensation package, don't forget other monetary and non-monetary priorities you would like included in the package. Analyze the fringe benefits, medical and any profit-sharing or retirement plans. Don't jump at accepting a job and then realize the benefits are not what you expected or need. Your leverage is highest after the offer is made but before you accept. You may arrange waivers of "non-negotiable" items which are important to you if you convince the employer of your value.

Don't forget non-monetary items such as the location of your office, funds available for decorating, and personal technology. Agree on any secretarial, assistant, or staffing needs, including the availability of other lawyers to assist you in your work.

At the equity partner level, obtain the firm financial reports. Have someone knowledgeable in law firm finances review the financials. You don't want to end up in a preventable situation by joining a firm with shaky or questionable finances.

Understand the capital requirements of the firm. How much money is required for a capital contribution? Are you expected to make payments up front, through draw reductions, or with borrowed funds? The compensation system should be understood, and all guarantees or other financial terms put in writing. Forward the partnership agreement and any other agreements you will sign to a lawyer for review.

ACCOUNTABILITY

To successfully revitalize your distressed career, you must set goals and take action to reach your objectives. A crucial part of your career revitalization action plan is to establish a system of accountability for keeping yourself committed to your action plan.

Everyone needs to be accountable to someone besides themselves, no matter how dedicated and motivated they may be. Accountability can be provided by someone in your family, a friend or a colleague. Or, a professional you've retained to assist in your distressed career revitalization. Professionals may be the best option to ensure your accountability to the career revitalization process.

ACCOUNTABILITY PARTNERS

Career revitalization is a continuing pursuit which you don't complete until you retire. It is easy to lose focus and momentum if you aren't diligent. This is true even if you aren't looking for another job. But, it is also true when seeking a new position. Once the initial burst of activity is over, many lawyers sit back and wait for the phone to ring. This is a problem.

It's hard to be disciplined and consistently hold yourself accountable. There are too many things occupying your attention, too many distractions, and too many things on your to-do list to be vigilant over some important, but not urgent, tasks. These are the tasks where there is no pressure to complete them – no deadline, no boss asking for a status report. These are also the important tasks which you need to complete to move you forward in creating your ideal career.

We all need accountability partners to ensure we focus on those important but not urgent tasks. I had to write a $10,000 check to a mentor to hold myself accountable for finishing this book. If I didn't produce the manuscript in six weeks, he would have cashed my check. If he had not pushed me to be accountable by urging me to write him a check in front of a mastermind group, you would not be reading this book. I may never have written it.

In most of our working lives, we are held accountable by partners, supervising counsel, or clients. That type of accountability means we will finish a task by a deadline (at least most of the time). But, it might not be the most important task we could work on in advancing our career.

When you work with an accountability partner, use someone who holds you accountable for deadlines you agree on. They also need to help you sort the urgent but unimportant tasks from the not urgent but important tasks so you can focus your efforts on important matters. Help with prioritizing your tasks can be at least as important as agreeing on and being held accountable for meeting deadlines.

WHO ARE YOUR ACCOUNTABILITY PARTNERS?

Outside of the partners we work with or our clients, we rarely have accountability partners. Some of you are disciplined enough to act as your own accountability partner, but few of us can do so consistently. While the most efficient productivity machines may work long hours and accomplish most tasks within a reasonable time, even those lawyers; need help in the prioritizing aspect of accountability.

What qualities should you look for in an accountability partner? You need someone who knows you well enough to see through your excuses and frustrations while remaining compassionate toward the demands on your time. Someone who can be emotionally removed enough to give you a kick in the pants when necessary, and a shoulder to cry on if needed. Someone who can help you identify those important but not urgent items you need to give priority to accomplishing. Someone with the ability and time to talk with you consistently.

Family, friends, or colleagues may be potential accountability partners. Family members, though, including spouses, can be tricky. In the role of an accountability partner, they need to be emotionally separated enough to not let their personal relationship with you interfere with their job as an accountability partner.

Friends or colleagues may also be potential accountability partners. Their ability to commit consistent time to talk with you may be an issue. The ability of friends to maintain emotional separation in this role may also be difficult. Be careful when using colleagues as accountability partners. It is tricky because of the need to keep information confidential and because of their potential bias related to your working relationship.

Professional consultants, advisers, and coaches are the best accountability partners. They can schedule regular times to talk as part of their work. They have the emotional distance to be tough if the situation demands it. They also possess the perspective to be effective in helping you sort out the important tasks that must be accomplished before you get lost in the urgent but unimportant tasks. The potential drawback is that, at the beginning of a relationship, these professionals don't know you, and that may limit their ability to be an immediately effective accountability partner. This is not a problem for long if it exists because these professionals are trained to be emotionally intelligent and present in order to pick up on your unique personality.

The most critical factors in working with an accountability partner are honesty, transparency, and full disclosure. If you are not upfront with your accountability partner and don't disclose all information to them, you are wasting both of your time, and it is counterproductive for you.

Find an accountability partner now. They will be invaluable in helping you move forward in your career revitalization process. They will help you prioritize and take action focused on finding the perfect job and ideal career. This will lead to your success, prosperity, and personal fulfillment.

MARKETING AND SALES (PERSONAL BRANDING & PROMOTION)

MARKETING AND SALES IN DISTRESSED BUSINESS TURNAROUNDS

Businesses must generate revenue in order to succeed. If the revenue cannot cover expenses, a business must liquidate.

Many successful business turnarounds are based on increasing revenue to attain profitability. To increase revenue, the business's clients must buy more of its services or the price of those services must be increased. Businesses' marketing and sales functions drive increased revenue.

Marketing identifies potential clients and makes them aware of the services offered by a business. Marketing also entices potential clients to become purchasers by showing them how the services can solve one of their problems. Additionally, marketing helps to establish trust in the business and its solutions.

A business's sales function is to consummate a transaction between the business and the client. Sales may also handle the customer service and customer retention functions.

MARKETING AND SALES IN A LAWYER'S DISTRESSED CAREER REVITALIZATION

Yep, you had a feeling I would get to this. I can already hear the chorus of, "I didn't become a lawyer to be a salesman."

I feel your pain. Today, though, there aren't too many careers where you don't market and sell yourself to succeed. And, the law is not an exception. Buck up, it's not that painful. You might even enjoy it.

No matter what your job or career path, you must market and sell yourself to succeed. This doesn't require you to be a sleazy used car salesman. Far from it.

Marketing your services is based on building a solid, professional foundation. You must establish credibility and trust within your target market, whether your market is potential employers or clients. You must promote yourself as the solution to one of your target market's problems.

To create your ideal career, you must sell yourself to others. The days of marketing and selling yourself once during law school to the highest bidder and then having a long and happy career are luxuries of the past.

Today, the most successful lawyers, in or out of law, are consistent marketers. Lawyers who do not market themselves soon find they are falling behind in their careers. Personal marketing is no longer optional; it is a necessity for success. Not to put too fine a point on it, but marketing and selling yourself is essential to your success, prosperity and personal fulfillment.

Personal branding is the cornerstone of professional service marketing. You need to position yourself as a knowledge expert in a particular service or industry, and learn everything about the problems in that service or industry. But, more than just being great at the technical aspect of your practice area is necessary. You must be able to offer customized solutions to potential employers' and clients' problems.

While you're developing your personal brand, you also must engage in promotional activities so people in your target market will come to know, like, and trust you. Your visibility increases as your target market learns that you solve problems which cause them to lose sleep. Buzzwords, boasts, promises, slick brochures, and fancy dinners are not enough.

If your personal branding and promotion are strong, selling is easy. At some point, potential employers and clients in your target market will approach you with little sales effort being required on your part.

See, no used car salesman here. The golden key – offer a solution to one of your target market's biggest problems. Then, take consistent action to make your target market aware of you and your ability to help them sleep better.

Whether your envisioned ideal career path involves working in a firm, as an in-house counsel, in government, or outside of the law altogether, you must establish and market your personal brand.

To succeed, or even to continue employment with a firm and move beyond an of-counsel level, you must build a client base of your own. Some lawyers may be very satisfied with working as an employee who earns a good salary, and avoids the pressures and responsibilities of equity partners. However, if your ideal career path includes advancing to equity partnership, and if you don't control a client base, you better have some incriminating photos of the managing partner.

If you are an in-house lawyer, you must also develop and promote your personal brand. Your target market is potential internal clients within the business units. People within the company must view you as a valuable resource, or you will be looking for another position soon. You must also promote yourself to other corporate counsel and key business leaders in your industry. You must build awareness of your existence, and a reputation for being credible and trustworthy in order to expand opportunities along your ideal career path.

"Okay Yates, my ideal career vision is to be a government lawyer. I get a pass on this marketing stuff, right?" Not so fast. Government lawyers must also market themselves to advance in their careers. Just like in-house counsel, internal clients must want to use your services for you to retain your job. Also, you need to be prepared to move up or move on.

If your ideal career points toward a position outside of the law, your personal branding and promotion strategies are even more important. In the law, you have at least the beginnings of a foundation to establish your personal brand. You already have experience providing a service, and with consistent action you will establish yourself as a knowledge leader. Outside of the law, personal branding will require much more work. But, the work will be well worth it if you are determined to realize your ideal career vision.

You can't anticipate when the perfect job will appear. If you don't take consistent action to allow your target market to get to know, like, and trust you, you won't hear about the position.

YOUR FOUNDATION

Marketing yourself is an important aspect of the career revitalization process. These activities must be done consistently, whether you are actively searching for your next perfect job or not. It is important that people who can help you advance on the path toward your ideal career know, like, and trust you. That is the purpose of personal marketing, and your personal marketing rests on your foundation.

Your foundation comprises:

- Your vision of your ideal employer and ideal clients.

- Knowing why people buy your services.

- Developing a personal brand.

Having your foundation in place allows you to be comfortable and confident when you hold yourself out to the world. Your foundation allows you to let others know who you are and what you stand for. You can't please everyone all the time. Don't even try. Know who you are. Engage in self-promotion activities so others can learn of your awesomeness and get to know, like, and trust you.

RVRP

The Red Velvet Rope Policy (RVRP) was articulated by Michael Port in his book, Book Yourself Solid. The RVRP is based on the concept that you should work with your ideal clients if you want to book yourself solid. Why? Because if you work with clients that are less than ideal, they drain your energy and won't allow you to do your best work for them or others. If you're not doing your best work, you won't find referrals, and your ideal clients won't want to work with you. It can turn into a downward spiral, with you working with less and less desirable clients and feeling worse and worse.

"Well," you reply, "That's great in theory. But, I need clients to advance my career. And, how does this relate to my career transition in the first place?" Yes, I agree this can be tough when you are not booked solid and you're recoiling at the thought of turning paying clients away, or even cutting clients loose. But, you must agree that there are certain clients who you love to work with, and who bring out the best in you. Your goal is to work with those clients. Sometimes you need to turn away or fire clients who are not ideal, so you have the time and energy to work with ideal clients. The transition can be tough.

Now, how does the RVRP fit into your career transition?

When you go through your career revitalization process, you uncover your purpose, passions, strengths, interests, and your envisioned ideal future. Your ideal future includes working with ideal employers and clients.

When you're in the earlier stages of your career, you may let the rope down a little to work with less than ideal employers or clients. You may decide it's best to find a particular type of experience, work in a specific industry, or find exposure to certain people who are less than your ideal employer or client. That's fine if it's an intentional decision based on your long-term goals to realize your ideal career.

If you lower the rope to take your next position without considering how it fits into your long-term career strategy, though, you will hinder your efforts to create your ideal career. If you settle for the next opportunity that arises, no matter how good a fit it is with your vision of the perfect job, you will impede your efforts to create your ideal career. Settling will drain your energy and lead to a negative mental and emotional state. Sure, there are going to unpleasant situations and employer and client interactions during your career. But, don't go into a situation without a set intention of how you will use it to move your career forward.

The lesson of the Red Velvet Rope Policy is that there are certain employers and clients you were meant to serve, and others, not so much. Gravitate to those employers and clients who you were meant to serve and who bring out the best in you. Do your best to disassociate yourself from situations that will drain your energy, frustrate you, and lead to you doing less than your best work. Life's too short.

WHY PEOPLE BUY WHAT YOU'RE SELLING

Why do employers or clients "buy" the services you are selling? Why do employers hire you or clients retain you? Those questions are at the crux of your efforts to find the perfect job and create your perfect career. Those questions are at the root of any business's success, and even underlie most personal relationships.

Why does someone or some organization want to associate with you? Can you answer that question? If not, it's time you learned the key to finding the perfect job and creating your ideal career.

People and organizations "buy" you because you help solve a problem they are confronting. You provide value by providing services that someone else needs. Those services may be explicit. "I need someone to handle a piece of litigation or a transaction for me." The services desired by others may also be implicit. They still need the litigation handled, and the transaction closed, but what they are satisfying is a need to retain a "name" firm or a lawyer from a T14 school. This is a crucial point which many lawyers don't appreciate. While you may be among the best lawyers in providing legal services, if you don't meet all the needs of a potential employer, you will not be hired. You can overcome not satisfying all the desires of a potential employer, but it's best to know their desires before you devise a plan to convince them you are right for the job.

Often, employers will not tell you what they want. Sure, there is a written a job description with qualification requirements. But, sometimes the most important factors in the hiring decision are nowhere to be seen. This frustrates potential candidates in two ways. First, although you may be qualified, the stated qualifications may not be that important, or even necessary for the successful candidate. Second, you are in the dark on what qualifications are most important. Tough situation, but you can deal with it.

Before you consider how to determine the actual qualifications an employer is looking for, consider this question: why aren't employers explicit about what they want to begin with? Several reasons. In larger organizations, the person making the hiring decision may not have written or even closely reviewed the job description and qualifications. They let Human Resources draft it or directed that the description and qualifications used five years ago be recycled. However, the biggest reason the written description and qualifications don't capture the reality of the job is . . . . you guessed it, the lawyers. Concerns about employment law issues intrude into job descriptions and qualifications, so they become fiction. You may not like this playing field, but you better know what it looks like when you play.

DEVELOPING A PERSONAL BRAND

Whether you consciously develop it or not, you have a personal brand. A personal brand comprises the information the world knows about you. Is your personal brand like Apple or Samsung or Microsoft? Each of those companies has a set of values, characteristics, and traits known to the world. Companies spend hundreds of millions of dollars on advertising and promotions in order to communicate those values, characteristics, and traits. Sometimes it sticks, and other times a company's actions and word of mouth from users of their products are even more influential in defining their brand.

What is your brand? You need not take any action to have a personal brand. It is what it is. When you went through the 360-degree evaluation, what you heard was your personal brand. Is it what you thought it was? Were there things you discovered that you were not aware of? Do you like your personal brand? Would it be different if you asked other people, perhaps people you don't know as well?

A clear picture of your personal brand is critical to your career revitalization. If you haven't done a thorough job in completing the work in the 360-degree evaluation, finish it now. Unless you know how the world and potential employers and clients see you, it's hard to assess what you need to do to burnish your personal brand.

Reshaping, revising, and refining your personal brand is an ongoing process that will continue throughout your career. Be intentional and focused on what you want your personal brand to be. Your brand should reflect your purpose, passions, strengths, interests, and vision of your perfect job and ideal career. You don't want your personal brand to be a studious and introverted academician when your ideal career path is to become a take-no-prisoners litigator. That extreme juxtaposition is unlikely. But, the more you develop and broadcast a personal brand in alignment your perfect job and ideal career, the better the chance you will realize them.

There are two main components to building your personal brand. The first is to decide on your brand. What you want to be known for. Preferably passions, interests and skills you've already developed. Continue to work on honing your strengths. The second component is making sure that your brand is accurately communicated to the world. That is where personal marketing comes into play. It is crucial to promote your brand so others come to know, like, and trust you. It's just as important as having the brand. There must be substance to your personal brand, but that is not enough. Unless others know of your brand, your personal branding efforts will be of little use.

Why is it important to have an intentionally developed brand and consistently communicate it to the world? Because it is much easier to find the perfect job when those in a position to help you already know who you are, and like and trust you. Not only will it be easier making career transitions, but you will also be the lawyer who hears about opportunities first. You may even be approached with opportunities before they become known publicly. Wouldn't it be nice if your career transitions appeared before you without your having to go search for them?

Your personal brand should be how you want the world to see you. You don't want to be known for taking depositions when you want a career as a trial lawyer. When your personal brand is not who you want to be, you will be miscategorized and it will be hard to change others' perceptions. Many legal careers have washed up on the rocks because a lawyer's personal brand did not match their perfect job and ideal career. These lawyers never did what they wanted to do in their careers. But instead, they stuck to doing the work the world believed was their brand. That can lead to a miserable existence.

Realize how your actions, particularly your public actions, affect your career path and the opportunities which are open to you. If your employer is pushing you down a path that doesn't feel right, resist with all your might. Early in your career, having varied experience is good. You don't always know what you will be good at or if you will like something until you try it. However, be attentive to situations where you are getting too much experience with a skill or in an area where you don't want to work. This is likely to occur when you excel at a particular skill. You will be asked to do more and more of that work. You are good at it, and can be depended on to do the job. You might even find satisfaction for the recognition and attention. But, if you are not comfortable going down that career path, the sooner you jump off, the better. Before your personal brand forms into something you don't want. It is much more difficult to change a brand after it is set in the public's consciousness than it is to build it with intention and forethought.

A good way to develop your personal brand is to study other people at a higher level who already have a similar brand to the one you want. What's their career history? What skills are most important for their brand? What personality traits are they known for? What organizations do they belong to? What ideas or causes do they support? How do they dress? Where do they live? Find out as much as you can about people with a personal brand similar to the one you would like. This research will help you discover the actions you can take to build your personal brand.

SELF-PROMOTION STRATEGIES

Self-promotion is an absolute necessity for lawyers to find their perfect job and create their ideal career. Even if you have the perfect job today, the world changes. The global economy may turn upside down again, as it did in 2008. Your employer may experience financial difficulties. A partner you worked with may make a lateral move and not invite you along for the ride. Stuff happens, and you need to be prepared. Once you have your personal foundation and brand in place, schedule consistent time for self-promotion activities.

When I discuss self-promotion, I'm not talking about slimy used car sales techniques, robo-callers, or infomercials. Self-promotion techniques for lawyers are aimed at driving awareness of you and the services you offer. Self-promotion is not ego-driven or boastful. Self-promotion strategies create awareness of you, and give others the opportunity to like and trust you. These activities will make selling yourself or your services easier when the time comes, or may even prompt an unsolicited sales conversation.

Six self-promotion strategies are available for lawyers. Three are mandatory: networking, direct contact, and referrals. The other three, writing, speaking, and online strategies are optional, although every lawyer should be on LinkedIn and have a complete profile.

Networking refers to keeping in touch with people who you already know and nurturing those relationships by providing value. Direct contact is meeting people you don't know and developing relationships with them. Referral combines networking and direct contact, on autopilot. You engage a select group of people in your network to connect you with people you don't know in order to help you make new connections and form new relationships.

Writing can be used both online and offline. There are many venues where you can use public speaking as a self-promotion strategy. Online self-promotion strategies can take many forms. You can create a personal website, blog, or use LinkedIn, Facebook or Twitter. The only necessity for online self-promotion is that all lawyers must have a complete LinkedIn profile and update it regularly.

NETWORKING

"Networking."

Yep, that word again. Most lawyers recoil from it. Thoughts of mindless chatter at endless cocktail parties with people shoving business cards at each other. Enough to make you want to never hear the word again.

I understand. I hate that version of networking too. It's not even effective.

Networking is not about going to more events, joining more associations, or doing more lunches. It might include some of those things, or maybe not. Networking is more a mindset than a particular activity.

Networking is connecting with other people and providing value. I can hear you now, "What? What about me? I thought networking was about me getting job leads, referrals, clients, and inside information from other people." Yes, you are right. But only because you provide value to other people first.

"Huh, how do I do that?" You network by being authentic and expressing yourself to others with the goal of serving them. It is easy to meet and get to know others if the focus is on them, and not you. Most everyone wants the focus to be on them – the "what's in it for me" mentality. If you have a mindset of serving others by giving value, you are golden. You will be inducted into the Networking Hall of Fame. Success, prosperity, and personal fulfillment will be abundant in your career and life.

"Wow!" Big promises, but why? Because, when you possess a mindset of service to other people, they will flock to you and want to help you. It's the reciprocity principle at work. If you give something to someone, they have an emotional response that prompts them to return the favor. Most of us want to help other people who have helped us. "Give and ye shall receive."

"Well, isn't this all too calculated?" It can be. If your desire to provide value to others is done with the expectation of immediately receiving something in return, it is not authentic. Others will see through you and realize you are a calculating poser. They will intuitively sense you are a charlatan.

The key to networking is to approach it with an authentic mindset of service to other people. Yes, you hope that some may be in a position to help you and will do so. But the first principle of networking is to focus on others first. Put yourself in their shoes. Be empathetic.

How do you develop a mindset of service? You listen. Listen with a genuine interest in others. Hear what they are saying.

Show a real interest in others and they will tell you how you can serve them. They may not say what they need directly, but if you are paying attention, they will say something that will give you clues. Follow up with thoughtful questions to help clarify and refine others' needs. Once you grasp their needs, it is much easier to identify something you can provide that will be valuable to them.

One of people's biggest needs is to be listened to with empathy. They need to "bend your ear" or have a "shoulder to cry on." The best networkers are not the life of the party. Those people regaling a crowd with their stories and jokes. Nope, the most effective networkers are found in quiet individual conversations or with a small group, listening to others. Just the act of empathetic listening may be enough to give value to other people and establish a closer connection with them.

Many lawyers tend toward the introversion side of the personality scale. While these lawyers may believe they can't be good networkers, this is far from accurate. Extroverts may seem like natural networkers, and some are superb at it. But extroversion does not determine networking success. What determines networking success is the ability to listen empathetically. Extroverts talk more than introverts, by definition. When talking, you are not listening. Contrary to popular belief, introverts are better at networking because they listen more than many extroverts.

Whether you are an introverted or extroverted lawyer, in networking, you must listen attentively and with empathy. For introverts, listening without paying attention because you are looking for the quickest way to escape the conversation is not effective. For extroverts, half-listening while planning how to set up your next story is also ineffective.

What can you give to others? Yourself, your time, your experience. People like to make their lives easier. How can you help them? By being attentive and intentional. Is there a piece of information that may be useful to someone? Could you pass along a blog post, article, website, app, or news story? Did you discover an excellent restaurant, tailor, shop, or kids' playground you could pass along?

Consistency is critical to effective networking. Consistent action creates a networking habit and leads to a networking mindset. With a networking mindset, you don't think about networking – it is just something you do and someone you are.

To become consistent, start by blocking out ten minutes on your calendar every day; do it in the morning, so there's less temptation to skip it. What can you do in ten minutes, early in the morning? Go to your LinkedIn profile. Check the "People you know" box to the right of your name to see if any of your contacts has a birthday, work anniversary, or a new job. Write them a short two or three sentence message of congratulations. Then go to Facebook and send a brief message to your connections with birthdays. In ten minutes, you can connect with five to ten people.

How are you serving people by sending them quick messages on their work anniversary, birthday, or job change? You are not only giving people attention and recognition, which most people crave, but you are also reminding them of your presence in the world. You may offer a service they need, but they've forgotten you exist. Now, you've reminded them if they need that service. Keep top of mind with your contacts.

As a bonus, anyone else that comments on a LinkedIn event can also see your comment. Since you are linked through the person you sent a message to, you may also trigger a top-of-mind moment for the other people commenting.

Another excellent way to network is to forward posts, articles, and news stories that might interest one or more of your connections. If you are surfing the web and want to forward the item, then do it. If not convenient or efficient use the Evernote browser plug-in to save the material to send out later. Then, at a scheduled time, send a group of transmittal emails.

People are inundated with so much information they appreciate it when someone sends them something interesting that is tailored just for them. Even if they already saw the item, you've created social capital by your action. You need to be intentional and thoughtful in this process. Don't send random articles or self-promotional material with little informational value. That will peg you as a spammer, not an effective networker.

While social media and email are great ways to network with only a small time commitment, personal conversations add tremendous weight to your networking. Instead of, or besides, sending an article or forwarding news with an email or through social media, pick up the phone.

Have a purpose when you make a networking call. Even if it is just to say something like, "wanted to make sure you were interested in the type of email I sent you." Or, "just stumbled across your name when searching my contact list and called to see what you've been up to lately." Whatever the reason, make sure it is about the other person. Only about the other person. If you go into the conversation with a suppressed agenda, it won't build your social capital.

When you call someone, and they don't answer, leave a message. The message should be short. But, leave your name and number, and the reason you called. If it is more of a stay-in-touch networking call, let the other person know that, although you left your number, you don't expect a call back. Something like, "No need to call back, but let's catch up soon." That way, you become top of mind while relieving the other person of the obligation to call you back. You set the stage for another call to them in a few weeks.

Even better than a call is an in-person conversation. These discussions solidify relationships. Your purpose is to build social capital by going deeper in the relationship. You have more time to explore ways you can serve the other person when face-to-face. You are establishing both professional and personal bonds. Be intentional in arranging the conversations. Have something you believe will be of value before scheduling. The value should not be something you are selling – at least, not at this meeting. It may be a fine line, but don't sell at these meetings; instead, inform.

If you closed several big hotel transactions recently, invite a real estate investor contact to lunch. Don't sell your legal services. Instead, talk about what you see in the real estate market, news of any of the players, and changes in standard contract terms. This information is of genuine value to a real estate investor.

At this point, don't ask if your contact is looking for legal services, an in-house counsel, or someone to help on the business side. Listening and providing helpful information is sufficient. You can have a sales conversation at a later point if appropriate. This meeting is about the other person, not about you. If they ask or inquire about your services, by all means respond, but don't bring it up first.

Conserve time and maximize the effectiveness of your networking efforts. One-on-one lunches and dinners are time consuming. Try to maximize the impact of these commitments. Schedule them with people who are most likely to assist you in finding the perfect job and ideal career. If you're thinking about making a lateral move, go to lunch with a senior partner in your practice area at another firm, not your son's baseball coach. You can talk to your son's baseball coach at games or drop by his store; you might discover he is best friends with the managing partner of another firm. But, schedule your face-to-face meetings in a way designed to better leverage your time.

Always be looking for ways to help others. This requires no significant time commitment. It is the little things that will pay big rewards in the networking game. A quick email with a news item not likely seen by your contact. A short call to congratulate someone on a work anniversary. A recommendation for an excellent new Argentinian restaurant.

DIRECT OUTREACH

Direct outreach is distinguished from networking because, when networking, you are already connected with the other person. In direct outreach, you don't know the person you are attempting to connect with. Once you connect with someone by direct outreach, and establish even a weak connection, that person will move into your network.

Build a list of people you would like to know. People who peak your interest. People in positions that might be helpful to you along your ideal career path. People who are knowledge leaders in areas related to your career. Continue to add to this list as you learn about people from online sources, hear about them from other people, or read their work. Be focused and intentional about adding people who may help you to find the perfect job and create your ideal career.

Once you identify someone you would like to meet, you need a plan for how to make that happen. The first thing you must do is research the person. Find out everything you can about them. With the online resources available today, you will able to find out a good deal of information about almost anyone. Google them. Look at their LinkedIn profile. Check out their Facebook profile and Twitter feed, and any other social media they are on.

Brainstorm ways to meet. Do you know someone who knows them? Check LinkedIn by searching the person you would like to meet and seeing if you have any first or second-degree connections in common. A personal introduction is always the best way to meet someone. You will get a little trust just from the introduction. A common connection establishes a basis for starting a conversation. The stronger your connection's relationship is with the person you would like to meet, the better.

Approach the mutual connection and tell them why you want to meet this person. You can either email or call your mutual connection, depending on your relationship. You hope your contact will offer to make an introduction. If not, ask them for the introduction. Tell your connection what you will request from their contact. There is no better way to ruin relationships than to get an introduction to someone and then ask that person for big favors or large chunks of their time. The contact who introduced you will be embarrassed and will never introduce you to anyone again. Show respect for people who agree to make an introduction.

If you have no direct connection for an introduction, look for other ways to connect. Follow them on social media. Re-tweet, Forward, Like, or Comment on their LinkedIn, Twitter, or Facebook posts. If the individual has a blog, post a substantive comment. Don't be a stalker by commenting or liking everything they post.

See if you can determine what organizations they belong to. Check out LinkedIn and any websites. See if they mention anything about associations or meetings in their posts. If they post they are traveling to a specific city, check to see if any organizations they are likely to belong to are having meetings in the area.

If you can find no other way, cold call or send a blind email or letter. In a few sentences, describe why you would like to meet them. Mention any common interests. Suggest a short (five to ten minute) call to introduce yourself. Find something to offer as value to the person you would like to meet. Be creative. If you are from different generations, offer to give a quick insight into your generation. If you are in a different industry or are experienced in an area that might be of interest, offer to share your insights. The more thorough your research, the more likely you are to offer value to this person.

Direct outreach for self-promotion may take time to implement with certain people. The higher the status of the person, the harder it is to connect. You might connect with someone at a lower or similar status level as yours on your first cold call. But, if the person is at a much higher status level, it may take months of concerted effort to connect.

Always be looking for opportunities to connect. When you are with friends or other contacts, mention the person you are trying to connect with. You would be surprised how often one of your personal contacts has a connection with an individual you are trying to meet.

Be persistent, but not annoying. It is a fine line sometimes. Know yourself and push past your usual inclination. If you are sometimes a little too persistent, pull back and don't make that sixth call when your five prior calls over two days weren't returned. If you're the type that hangs up after two rings and never calls back, leave several messages before you give up your cold calling campaign.

Do not rush into a relationship too quickly. This is just like dating – trying to rush someone to the altar on the second date is never a good idea. Take it slow. Search for opportunities to add value and develop the relationship. In the immediate post-direct contact stage, use more casual networking efforts like sending an article or recommending a restaurant.

After you make the direct contact and establish a relationship, you can move them into your networking process.

REFERRALS

You need to identify a small group of people from your current network of contacts to build referral relationships. These should be people that know you well, and who like and trust you. They are people who come in contact with your ideal clients.

Referral sources can promote you as a solution to problems of your potential clients. In building the referral relationships, make sure your referrers know what solutions you can provide.

Remember referral relationships are two-way. You must also provide value to the people in your referral network.

PUBLIC SPEAKING

Public speaking can be a useful for self-promotion for some lawyers. Many lawyers are public speakers as part of their work. They speak before courts or administrative tribunals regularly. These skills may develop into a practice of using public speaking as part of their self-promotional efforts.

Public speaking can be a powerful self-promotion strategy. Instead of connecting one-on-one like with networking and direct contract, you reach many people at one time. Unlike writing, there is an immediate connection with the people in your audience and it is much easier to show yourself as someone they can like and trust. You can tailor your message to the audience, something you can't do as well with your writing.

How do you become a public speaker? You do it. Explore opportunities to speak at every event you can. Start with your employer to get experience. Volunteer to give a lunchtime talk on some subject of interest. Explore whether the associations and professional organizations you belong to have speaking opportunities. You will not get the opening keynote or the big stage the first time out, but keep at it. As with all self-promotion strategies, consistency in your efforts is the most important factor in using public speaking to promote your personal brand.

What do you speak about? What are you interested in, and what topics will relate to your ideal career path? What topics is your audience interested in? You find an intersection between what you want to talk about and what your audience wants to hear. Your audience is always more important than you when you're a public speaker.

Brainstorm a few topics and jot down a few bullet points to turn into an outline. Is there enough information to develop a speech? It doesn't take too much work to put together an informal five-minute lunch presentation. It takes a tremendous amount of work to kill a forty-five-minute keynote address.

What type of speech are you going to give? Speeches are classified as either informational/teaching or as message/motivational speeches. Again, what your audience wants is the most important consideration. Are they looking to be informed or do they desire a message? Will you be teaching or motivating? You can take the same topic and material, and mold it into either type of speech.

Lawyers are typically more inclined to give an informational/teaching type speech. Mastery of substantive material can establish you as a knowledge expert. Most lawyers, the fiery closing argument orators excepted, feel more comfortable teaching as opposed to motivating. While many audiences want to learn, you make a closer emotional connection with a great message/motivational speech. Both types of speeches are important, but when someone is choosing a brand, the emotional wins over the intellectual if there is already trust on the substantive material.

Once you decide which type of speech to develop, how do you structure it? There are several good models. The formats are not mutually exclusive, and most speeches combine several formats within the structure of the speech.

You can use a numbered list of items to organize your material. For instance, "7 Habits of Highly Effective People." You can use a modular approach where there are several subtopics within your main topic, but the order you present them is not important. You can do a chronological speech where you start at a beginning and move through to the end. Speeches developed from war stories can follow this structure. You can do a problem/solution format where you pose several problems and then offer solutions.

When you decide on a structure, take your outline and write the speech by expanding the outline and fitting it into your chosen speech structure. The most important elements of a speech are the arc of the story, the energy of the presentation, and the contrasts exhibited during the speech.

Whatever the structure of your speech, try to incorporate a traditional hero's journey paradigm. Begin with the way the world looks now. Set the stage. Introduce the problem or issue being confronted. Provide the solution or resolution to the problem. Then, contrast how the world looks when the solution is achieved, and how it would look if no action were taken.

Energy and enthusiasm are contagious. Don't put your audience to sleep. You are responsible to your audience for bringing your energy and enthusiasm to the stage. Show it through your words, your voice, and your body movements. Don't try to be Tony Robins or Robin Williams – be yourself, but be your most energetic and enthusiastic self.

Contrast in your speech separates you from the average speaker. Remember, you are giving a performance, not just a speech. While you project energy and enthusiasm, during parts of the speech, you may be mellow and laid back. Use a period of quiet conversation with your audience. The tone, pitch, and volume of your voice must be modulated and vary during your talk. The words you use can help put contrast into the speech. In some places, there may be more formal words, and in other places more informal slang words. Your body movement also provides contrast. Sometimes you are up close to the edge of the stage. At other times, you are further back.

Tell a story with your speech. Show your energy and enthusiasm. And, incorporate contrast. These three things will make you a heroic public speaker.

Some public speakers like to speak extemporaneously, with a few bullet points to guide their talks. While this is fine for brief speeches, few public speakers possess the ability to give a polished speech of over five minutes when it hasn't been scripted. Yes, some can push through without a script, but most people taking this tact don't perform as well as they could.

Should you memorize your speech and deliver it word for word? No, you don't have to. Once your script is written and rehearsed repeatedly, you will develop confidence in your material. You will know the sections, how they fit together, and the flow of the speech. You will be confident because you know the material cold. Even if you skip a few sentences or deliver a few paragraphs out of order, you will know how to get back to the flow of the speech and continue your performance.

After you write your speech, you need to rehearse it. You need to speak the words as you would before an audience. Find a table to set your script on and read aloud. Don't just say it in your head – speak the words. See how it feels to you. Written and spoken speech can be different, so you may find that parts of your script seem stilted. You may need to rewrite portions of the speech in a more conversational way.

After you go through a few table reads of your speech, it is time to get it on its feet. Stand up and give the speech out loud. Don't do it in front of a mirror. You will be distracted by your appearance, and you will not have the same quality rehearsal. Although rehearsing in front of a mirror is fairly standard advice, don't do it.

As you rehearse, you will continue to revise your speech. The words you speak will come out more naturally and differ from the words on the paper. Pay attention to how your body moves during your speech, and become more intentional in how you move. Plan how you move and where you stand during different parts of the speech in order to produce maximum effect.

Continue rehearsing. You will be surprised at how much rehearsal time is necessary to give a great performance, as opposed to stumbling through your speech. Which do you want, an epic performance or a passable speech? Which establishes your personal brand better and is more useful for self-promotion?

It is difficult, and it takes considerable time, to become an excellent public speaker. But, the effort is worth it when you come off the stage and realize that you have captured the entire audience. You have established your personal brand with the audience while you were on stage. You can't build that emotional bond in such a short period and with so many people with any other self-promotion activity.

WRITING

Most lawyers write for a living. At least part of the time. Our masterpieces are not epic novels made into blockbuster movies, but the basis for granting a motion to compel or a spellbinding venue provision.

Since lawyers are writers, should you use writing as one of your self-promotion activities? "Maybe" is a good lawyerly answer. Writing is a great strategy for lawyers – just not the type of writing usually produced in the law. The only time you need to write the traditional scholarly articles for publication in journals is if you want to be an academician. Or, if you are looking for your first job as a lawyer. Otherwise, a lot of your time and energy is wasted on something that may get a footnote in a legal opinion, but little else.

What is your goal in writing for self-promotion? Like other self-promotion channels, it is to become known, liked, and trusted by your intended target audience.

Who is your intended target audience? What do they read? Where do they read? What subjects and topics interest them? These are the types of questions to answer before choosing a writing platform to publish your work. Publish your work where your intended target audience is likely to see it. Write on topics they want to read about.

If you write for self-promotion, you have many choices of platforms. You can write a several-sentence news update or alert, and post it in LinkedIn or Facebook updates. Longer pieces with news, opinion, or analysis can be posted on free platforms such as LinkedIn Pulse or Medium. You can create a personal blog, but that will require substantial work in promoting it to gain a reasonable number of subscribers and make your writing efforts worth your time.

If your employer has a blog, writing for it is a possibility, although it will be mainly, if not exclusively, geared toward promoting the employer and not you. You can also write guest posts for other blogs. Many websites are always searching for good writers to post to their sites. Traditional publications like legal magazines and general interest publications are now found in both print form and online. These publications provide other opportunities to write. And then the holy grail, publishing your writing as a book.

Wherever you publish, unless you control the platform, you need to get permission from the gatekeepers. This is one reason that publishing on LinkedIn, or your personal blog, is great, at least to start. You need no one's permission – just a computer and a few quite minutes to write. You then hit the publish button, and your writing is up on LinkedIn or your blog for the world to marvel at. If you guest blog or want to be published on someone else's website, you need an invitation to enter. Use your network to find connections with editors or bloggers that control the website's content. Use direct outreach to contact the individual gatekeepers and establish a relationship. Post on LinkedIn or other sites where you can publish without permission, and use that work as an example of what you can produce.

Publishing your work independently of your employer is my recommendation for maximum impact in self-promotion. You need to check to see if there are any issues you may have with publishing your writing outside of channels controlled by your employer. Don't write on company time or use proprietary information in your writing. Read any employment contract you may have, and any employee handbooks or manuals for information on restrictions on publishing your writing. Unless doing so is prohibited, my preference is to publish, and if questions are raised, ask for forgiveness and permission to continue at that time. Legal employers are conservative (hey, big revelation there, huh?). When you ask for permission, an instinctual response is "no." Cite your relationship with your employer in your biographic information on the post and state that your writing is only your personal opinion. Also, point out whether the employer has been involved in anything you're writing about. Otherwise, go forward and publish.

What should you write about? Write about whatever your intended target audience is interested in, not what you want to discuss. Writing for self-promotion is a marketing exercise. Marketing is not about you – it is about your audience. Your audience's wants and needs.

Write about current events. Write about problems confronting your audience. Write about your views on the future, or a specific current issue or trend. Be yourself. Express an opinion. Don't fear being controversial (but again, note in the publication these are your views and not those of your employer).

Most lawyers are conservative and logical, by-the-book writers. We may use big words and write in long sentences and paragraphs. These writing habits might be useful for writing briefs, although I question even that, but they are not good habits if you want to be read.

Write like a novelist or copywriter. Tell a story. Sell the soap. You want your audience to be engaged, to read more than the first few sentences, and to remember you.

Don't use fancy-pants words. Use short sentences and paragraphs. Use subheadings, bullet points, and numbered lists. Look at the popular writers in your field and your audience's field, and use some of the same writing devices they use.

You are writing to address your audience's needs and desires. To help them solve problems that keep them awake at night. You are also writing to establish a personal brand. Don't neglect either goal in your writing. If you find it tough to reconcile the two, look to see if something more is askew in the alignment between your target audience and your personal brand.

Writing can be a great self-promotion strategy for lawyers. Have fun, and remember you are not drafting a brief or a contract. Instead, your writing should aim to be more of a short story or a good piece of long-form copywriting.

ONLINE

Online self-promotion includes anything about you in digital form which is publically available. From websites to social media, from blogs to news articles. Information posted by you or about you.

The first thing you need to do is assess your current online presence. Do a Google search for your name. Also, do Bing and Yahoo searches. Go through the results and look at the first fifty results. Make sure there is no negative information lurking which you should know about.

Go to each item and make a note of the contents. Is it something like a LinkedIn or Facebook profile you control, or something like a news article or press release you don't control? Or, is it something like your employer's profile on its website, which you may have some control over?

Were you surprised at what you found? Were there negative items in the search results? Perhaps negative items on review sites? Or, were there only a few search results?

Clean up old out-of-date items which you control. Are your old Myspace or other social media accounts still active? Shut them down and delete them where possible. Do you have an Instagram or Pin Interest account you never use? Consider shutting them down and deleting them. You don't want to have old inactive accounts. It adds nothing to your personal brand and may rank higher in search results than something that is more relevant. Just because you delete the accounts doesn't mean the search results will go away, but they will move down in rankings.

Now that you have assessed what is already online, it is time to decide if you want to use social media as part of your online self-promotion strategy. Being online for self-promotion takes time. Even if you use Twitter, those 140-word tidbits take time to compose. If you use online activities for self-promotion, you will need to commit to spending the time required to do it well. You need to consistently use the platform by posting, publishing, or otherwise pushing out new content in order for your efforts to be effective for self-promotion. You also need to spend the time to interact on your chosen platform. It is called "social" media.

What do you hope to accomplish online? For most lawyers, their online self-promotion objective is to let others know about, like, and trust them. Being online is a method of letting others know about you, but only if you actively promote yourself. Posting on Twitter or Facebook about your favorite team or restaurant is not a strategy. Having a blog and posting three times a year is not a strategy. It is counterproductive to establishing a strong personal brand. If a potential employer finds your blog and sees you rarely post, they may conclude you are not a thought-leader, and that you don't follow through on your work.

LINKEDIN

One essential place every professional must have a presence online is LinkedIn. You must have a complete, well thought-out profile and photo to reflect your personal brand. Every word in your profile should be focused on your personal brand, how you want to be seen in the world, and on the perfect job and ideal career. You don't want people to have to guess who you are or where you want to go in your career.

Many lawyers use LinkedIn as an online resume. It is not a resume, though – far from it. You will lose a great opportunity to establish your personal brand if you treat your LinkedIn profile as a resume.

Besides having a complete profile, you can attach examples of your work. You can show articles you have written, videos or slides from speeches you have given, and other types of self-promotional media.

Also, think about regularly posting on LinkedIn. You can post short comments or links to interesting and relevant articles, whether yours or other peoples', in the update box. You can also use LinkedIn Pulse to publish long-form posts. The posts can be of any length, although shorter articles are viewed more often. Using this feature of LinkedIn is like having your own blog, but without the responsibility for maintaining a site and with a built-in audience for your posts from day one.

Every time you post on LinkedIn Pulse all of your first-degree connections receive notification within LinkedIn. If you post on LinkedIn Pulse, your words have the possibility of being seen by a much larger audience than your first-degree connections. If your posts are liked and commented on, or are featured in one of LinkedIn's categories, you may be exposed to thousands of lawyers. And, it's not unusual to get featured in one of LinkedIn's categories.

Giving and getting recommendations on LinkedIn is a powerful way to establish social proof of your personal brand. It is quicker to give and receive recognition for specific skills, but a personal recommendation is much stronger evidence of your brand.

OTHER ONLINE SELF-PROMOTION

Let's now look at various other ways you can use your online presence as part of your self-promotion strategy.

What social media services do you use? Which ones are for personal use and which ones do you use for business?

Any social media accounts for your personal use should have the security settings adjusted so that only a restricted group of people can see the posts. Do you have a Twitter account, but only for personal use? Consider locking it so only those people you allow to follow you have access to your tweets. Same with Facebook or other services. Twitter, Facebook, and other social media accounts can help personalize your brand to someone checking you out online (and everyone does). Don't post to public accounts unless you would be fine with it being on the front page of the New York Times. Even if a post is sarcastic or a joke, what you believed was innocuous at the time could come back to haunt you and your professional brand. Be careful, thoughtful and intentional online.

TWITTER

Twitter may be the quickest social media platform to use. You are limited to 140-word posts. Twitter is an ineffective self-promotion channel for most lawyers, though. If you use Twitter in your self-promotion strategies, you need to have a consistent and well thought-out posting strategy. Those 140-word tidbits will take time to post if you are thoughtful and intentional in your strategy. You also need to expand your follower list. You need followers who you interact with in order for Twitter to be an effective online channel for self-promotion.

Twitter lists are a great feature even if you don't use Twitter in your self-promotion efforts. They can help you stay up to date with specific subjects and with thought-leaders in your area. Use Twitter lists to categorize people who tweet so you can view all their posts together. Lists are a subset of the Twitter feed. You don't have to be following someone to put them on a list. You can create lists of your own or subscribe to lists others have already created.

By using lists, you can keep up with posts from a specific group of people. You can have a list of thought-leaders in particular areas so you can monitor what is happening. You can have a list of potential employers so you stay up to date on their latest news and rumblings. Create your personalized lists to help you stay on top of areas you are interested in. Search Twitter for keywords to find Twitter accounts that are relevant, and compile your lists from there.

FACEBOOK

Facebook is the big kahuna of social media platforms. Should you use Facebook as part of your self-promotion strategy? Probably not as a general strategy, but participating in active Facebook Groups is a good way to become known.

Search for Facebook Groups in areas where you would like to spread your personal brand. Look at the activity in a group. Are there many members? Are there regular posts? Do people leave comments? Are more than a few people active? If so, join the group, and have a scheduled time to look at the posts and participate in the discussions where relevant.

OTHER SOCIAL MEDIA

Outside the big three of LinkedIn, Twitter, and Facebook, for the vast majority of lawyers, other social media platforms are not relevant for their self-promotion strategies. While Instagram, Pin Interest, Periscope, Blab and other social media platforms may interest you, only a few lawyers will find them useful as part of their online self-promotion strategy.

WEBSITE - YOUR OWN

Should you have a personal website? If you're in Big Law, not unless you are a prolific writer who will produce content regularly. If you're a solo practitioner or are considering transitioning into a smaller practice or leaving the law, seriously consider building a personal website. You control your personal brand on your website. It can be a great way to present your personal brand.

If you are considering a website, what is the purpose? Who would you like to attract to the site? What do you want those people to do once they find to your site?

Many lawyers have personal websites. But these websites are typically little more than a glorified glossy brochure. While this type of site may be necessary for a sole practitioner or small firm as an online yellow pages listing, it is seldom useful for other individual lawyers. The work involved in setting up the site and in continued maintenance, and the continuing hosting and other fees, don't justify the minimal exposure such a site provides. Unless you have a site that is regularly updated, optimized for SEO, and promoted through other channels, very few people will ever find it.

Using LinkedIn as your online home base is a much better alternative to a personal website for most lawyers. It's free, efficient to use, and effective in attracting interested and relevant visitors.

If you decide to have a website as part of your personal branding, purchase a website domain name. Try to get your own name. If you have a common name, consider using your middle initial or another variation of your name. If available, purchase it even if you don't plan on creating a personal website. You never know when you might decide to build one. If you are building a personal brand around a particular skill, industry, or problem solution, try to find a name that reflects your brand. Although there are now many extensions, a dot-com extension is still the gold standard and the most widely recognized. If you plan on continuing to practice law, and the dot-com is not available, you might use your name and a dot-lawyer extension.

Unless you have the skills and experience to build your own website, you want to find professional help. The most important factors in building a website are a modern look and feel, ease of use for your visitors, and ease of use for you to update and post to the site. A good website can be built with relatively modest expenditures. Be careful because there are many people and companies that will charge you much more than you need to spend and produce inferior results. Get recommendations from people you know and look at websites that anyone you are considering hiring has built in the past.

CHAPTER 8

INFORMATION TECHNOLOGY (PRODUCTIVITY & REFLECTION)

INFORMATION TECHNOLOGY SYSTEMS IN DISTRESSED BUSINESSES

Information technology systems are essential to successful businesses. These systems range from simple accounting ledgers, kept in a journal or on a laptop, to sophisticated computer systems that process vast amounts of data.

Corporate turnaround professionals use information technology systems extensively. The professionals need data – and the information revealed by the data – to accurately assess a distressed business. They also use these systems to monitor the effectiveness of their turnaround efforts.

A common characteristic of distressed businesses is the lack of relevant information technology systems. The two most important aspects of a useful information technology system are the consistency of the data put into the system and the system's ability to produce timely and relevant information.

The challenge for any business is to focus on the most relevant information needed to analyze and help spot the best opportunities, and to discoverer problems before they become big issues. Corporate turnaround professionals add value by helping develop and install information technology systems capable of providing the information promptly.

INFORMATION TECHNOLOGY SYSTEMS IN A LAWYER'S DISTRESSED CAREER REVITALIZATION

You can use information technology systems and the data they produce to help you revitalize your distressed legal career. The information technology systems for personal use are software programs, apps, internet services, and journaling practices.

APPS, SOFTWARE, AND INTERNET SERVICES

There are software programs, apps, and internet services available for just about every area of your career and life. The most useful tools for your career revitalization are those relating to your finances, networking, personal branding, and self-promotion.

Use budgeting software to keep track of your finances and for help in setting your priorities. Budgeting software programs, apps, and internet services allow you to sort and analyze your financial data. Many also enable you to leverage the power of the internet to automate compilation of data from different sources without having to input the data manually.

Your networking efforts will be much easier to manage with software programs, apps, and internet services. While Outlook is still fine for many purposes, newer and more specialized services are now available to help you manage your contacts and be more productive in your networking efforts. These services consolidate information about all of your contacts in one place. The services also provide updated information from social media, and a semi-automated system to allow you to stay in touch with your contacts.

Some of your personal branding and self-promotion efforts can be more efficient if you use specialize software, apps, or internet services. There are many services available to collect and analyze data about your branding and self-promotional efforts. From Google Analytics to LinkedIn analytic tools, you can monitor the effectiveness and efficiency of the branding and self-promotion efforts on your website, blog, and social media channels.

Use apps, software programs, and internet services to assist you in keeping track of your tasks, calendar, research, and other information and data. These apps, programs, and internet services will help you be more effective, efficient, and productive in all areas of your life, not just in your career. By being more effective, efficient, and productive, you will have more energy and time to devote to implementing the career revitalization process.

It is important not to get caught up in the shiny new object syndrome that can occur when you discover new apps, programs, and internet services. The most important thing to remember when considering which tools to use is the purpose. What are you trying to accomplish? How will the app, software, or internet service help you? What are the benefits, and do they outweigh the time or cost involved in becoming proficient in their use? Will you use them? I'm a gadget junkie, and it is impossible to count the number of apps, programs, and other tools I have tried, bought, and even used for a short period, but then never used again. The money and time I wasted trying to be effective, efficient, and productive is mind-boggling.

Simplicity, ease of use, and a flat learning curve are the most important factors to consider after you decide that an app, program, or internet service will help you be more effective, efficient, or productive. If it's not simple, and easy to use and learn, there is a much greater chance you will never use it. While many features and capabilities are selling points you will only use a small fraction of the functionality of more comprehensive and feature-rich apps, programs, and tools unless you are using them to solve multiple issues.

JOURNALING AND PLANNING

One of the more important personal information technology practices for many lawyers is journaling, and periodic reviews. Good old-fashioned information technology.

Journaling is a fantastic productivity practice, and helps with both stress management and emotional regulation. The act of writing regularly can be cathartic and provide great insight. I recommend keeping a paper journal instead of keeping one on a computer because it seems more intimate, and there is a more direct connection to your brain. If you want to access the journal electronically, try one of the digital pen writing solutions so you can download the journal to your computer.

Schedule five to ten minutes in the early morning or evening, or both, to take out your pen and paper, and write about what is on your mind. Note your successes and your frustrations. Jot down any ideas or thoughts that surface. Many lawyers find it is a good practice to journal at the end of their work day as a mini-review and planning session. They review their day for unfinished tasks, and make a quick note of the most important items they will accomplish the next day. When they conclude their journaling, many then go to their calendar and schedule the most important tasks for the next day. This practice almost always shows up on lists of practices followed by the most productive and successful people.

A regularly scheduled weekly review is another practice of highly productive people. Schedule a regular time to review, reflect, and plan. Time to review what went well and what you need to work on improving the following week. Time to resolve open items, clean up your calendar, and schedule your activities for the next week. The practice pays big dividends. Depending on your schedule, a Friday afternoon, Saturday morning, or Sunday evening are all good times for a weekly review. The amount of time is not important. What is important is that you do the weekly review consistently.

Many lawyers also find a quarterly plan to be helpful. A quarterly plan helps you see where you want to go and how you will get there over a manageable time horizon. It is also a good time to look back at your prior quarterly plan. Review it to see how far you have advanced and note any areas you might need to pay more attention to in the following quarter.

Quarterly plans should be structured according to your own situation. Look at your strategic plan, goal list, and action plan. What are the most important goals you want to achieve in the next quarter? Look at goals not only in your current job, but in your life, and specific objectives related to your career revitalization. Do you want to find two new clients next quarter, lose 20 pounds, or implement your career revitalization plan?

List all the sub-goals you need to achieve in order to reach your primary goals for the next quarter. Then, list all the action items you will need to do to accomplish those objectives. Prioritize your goals, sub-goals, and action items. Get out your calendar and schedule your action items. Push yourself, but don't over-commit and over-schedule. It is much better to have flex-time built into your schedule than to stress yourself over not completing the items you have scheduled.

AFTERWORD

Your career is a business. The methods, techniques, tools, and strategies used by corporate turnaround professionals to revitalize distressed businesses apply to your job and career. This is true whether your vision of the perfect job and ideal career path is in the law or outside of the law.

The most important thing to remember is that information and knowledge are not enough. You will only revitalize your distressed career if you take action – consistent, focused action! My wish for you is to take action now to revitalize your distressed legal career.

Career revitalization never ends. There may be quiet periods where you are focused on your work and personal life, when you have the perfect job, and believe you are on your ideal career path. However, it is best to not totally neglect your career revitalization strategic plan, goal list, and action plan.

Even if your career and life are great, you still must devote time to activities focused on your personal brand and self-promotion strategies. The old saying, "dig the well before you need the water," is applicable. To achieve your ideal career, you want to continually increase the number of people that know, like, and trust you. You want to develop relationships with people through your networking, direct contact, and referral strategies.

Also periodically review the work you did on your purpose, passions, strengths, interests and vision. The world changes, you change. You may need to revise your thinking and work-sheets as you evolve. If there are revisions, you may also need to revise your strategic plan, goal list, and action plan. You will not need to go through this process often, but schedule the time to do it every couple of years.

If you have a significant life event such as getting married, having children, moving, or you have a major illness (yours, or that of a close family member), that may be a good time for a comprehensive review and update of your career revitaliza-tion process and plans. You may also want to do this full review if there is a significant event with your employer, the industry, or in your practice area. Your employer's financial troubles and disruptions, and increased competition in your industry, should trigger a comprehensive review. I hope you can better sense these major events before they occur once you have been through the career revitalization process. Then, you can revise your career revitalization strategic plan, goal list, and action plan before your next career transition.

As you go through your career on your ideal career path, taking the steps suggested by the career revitalization process laid out in this book should become second nature. You will de-velop habits that lead to actions designed to keep you on your ideal career path. You will have devised systems to boost your effectiveness, efficiency, and productivity to stay on top of your game and remain headed toward achieving your ideal career.

Just like a shark in the water (insert your own lawyer joke here), once you stop moving forward, you are dead. You only want that to occur after achieving your ideal career, and living a long and happy life with much success, prosperity, and personal fulfillment.

Happy trails. And, don't forget to write.

APPENDIX

This Appendix includes additional information and resources to help you work through and implement the career revitalization process in order to find the perfect job and create your ideal career.

The first section of the Appendix is a series of lawyer revitalization and transition scenarios. Lawyer career path transitions are discussed. Portions of the lawyer career revitalization process are shown to illustrate how they would be applied in typical lawyer career transitions.

The second section discusses lawyer job search sites and how to use them, if at all.

The third section includes other resources and references. The materials in this section change rapidly and are subject to regular revision. To keep the resources and references current, I have put them on my website at gregyatesconsulting. com/resources. The site will be updated, supplemented, and enriched regularly.

You can find PDF and Word versions of a workbook containing the questions exercises in this book, along with additional material, for download at gregyatesconsulting.com/professional-prosperity-for-lawyers.

APPENDIX I:
TRANSITION SCENARIOS

In this section, I discuss different scenarios where a lawyer is considering a career transition.

- A Big Law associate climbing the ladder to Big Law equity partnership.

- A Big Law attorney leaving Big Law.

- A lawyer moving in-house.

- A lawyer looking at New Law opportunities.

- A lawyer leaving the law.

These scenarios are about lawyers aligning their purpose, passions, strengths, interests, and vision with their perfect job and ideal career.

RAISING THROUGH THE RANKS IN BIG LAW

You've been a Big Law associate for a few years. You may have advanced to senior associate, counsel, or even non-equity partner. You sense that your career path may be topping out at the firm. But, you don't know where you stand on the firm's equity partnership track. You don't even understand the requirements to advance to equity partner.

Still, you still want to become a Big Law equity partner. But you're stuck, stressed, depressed, and getting desperate. What now?

First, take a deep look at yourself and your motivation for wanting to become a Big Law equity partner. Is it for the money, status, or other gifts and prizes you associate with Big Law equity partnership? Or are you passionate about practicing law and the work you do every day? Do you realize what an equity partner's life is like? Are you clear about the rewards, responsibilities, and obligations of being an equity partner? Do you appreciate the reality of the life of a Big Law equity partner?

You need to think about and answer these questions honestly if you want to become a Big Law equity partner. The path to equity partnership is difficult, and the demands once you get there are substantial. Before you spend every last breath you have to get the prize, be convinced the rewards will be worth it for you.

Convinced you want to be a Big Law equity partner? Great. Let's do it!

There is one magical, marvelous, mystical key to becoming a Big Law equity partner. And if you don't already realize the key, look at other career options.

The key is to do great work, right? Yeah, that's a minimum prerequisite, but you know the real key. Have your own clients. Don't look shocked. The top status and rewards in any business – and the law is a business – go to those who generate the most revenue for the business.

Your primary value to equity partners, the people who decide on your elevation to equity partnership, is the business you control and bring into the firm. You may be valuable because you are a great lawyer or because you can organize and manage legal work and client relationships. But, you will not become an equity partner without having your own clients. Period. End of story.

Yes, there are exceptions. More in the past than today. And those equity partners without significant business are being asked to leave the partnership. If you want to put all of your chips for becoming an equity partner on how great you are at practicing law, managing deals or cases, and working with clients, good luck. You'll need it.

If the key to becoming a Big Law equity partner is having clients, how do you find them?

You attract clients by recognizing their problems and making potential clients aware that you are the solution.

That's simple, right? You can litigate the pants off other lawyers. Or, you are the best deal jockey in town. Wrong! Attracting clients is not about you. It is not about what services you provide or how skilled you are at providing those services.

Attracting clients is all about the potential client. You must learn about the problems faced by the potential client, and understand the context of their problems. You must be able to solve their problems. Clients aren't interested in your exceptional generic services. Clients need customized solutions to satisfy their needs, wants, and desires. Then, the potential client must know, like, and trust you before they become your clients.

You will market and sell yourself, not your firm. Clients hire lawyers, not firms. There are few firms left where the majority of their clients are firm clients and will stay firm clients. Even if the lawyers servicing most of their matters leave the firm. Today, clients follow lawyers, not firms.

Another reason to market and sell yourself is that you want clients to be yours, not the firm's. At some stage, you may move your practice to another firm. You need clients to follow you. You don't need clients who you service, but who you are unsure of whether they will follow you if you move.

You will be most prepared to attract clients when you know what type of client is your ideal client. What problems do they grapple with every day? What industries are they in? Where are they located? What is their culture?

Consider clients you work with and identify your favorite clients. If you are trying to develop a client base, you will have more energy when you work with ideal clients. Once you've identified your ideal client, learn everything you can about potential clients matching your requirements. Learn about the companies, the industry, and the people in those companies.

As you are learning about those potential clients, develop your personal brand. Get clear on who you are and what you offer. You do not offer litigation or deal skills – you offer specific expertise and solutions. Become a knowledge leader in an area important to your ideal client. By your being a knowledge leader, potential clients will learn of you.

How do you become a knowledge leader? By knowing an area well, and offering ideas and information to help potential clients solve their problems. Once you prepare yourself, you are ready to promote your solutions.

How do you promote yourself? By having a strategy to initiate, develop, and build relationships with potential clients. You need to have a consistent plan to network with people you know. If potential clients know, like, and trust you, they will retain you when the need arises. They will also refer you to other potential clients.

You need to identify key people who can be helpful in your efforts to find clients. These people may be in-house counsel or other executives at potential client businesses. They may be industry experts or other lawyers who work for these ideal clients. And, they may be top members of related trade associations, or members of the press who report on your ideal client and its industry.

Once you've identified key people, think of ways to get an introduction or otherwise make them aware of you. Review your current contacts for possible introductions. Participate in industry trade associations. Follow them on social media and connect with them through commenting on their posts.

You also need to identify a small group of people from your current network of contacts to build referral relationships. These should be people that know you well, and who like and trust you. They are people who come in contact with your ideal clients. Referral sources can promote you as a solution to problems of those potential clients. In building the referral relationships, make sure your referrers know what solutions you can provide. Remember referral relationships are two-way. You must also provide value to the people in your referral network.

Some lawyers find public speaking helpful in promoting their personal brand and allowing potential clients to become aware of them. For most practices, speaking to groups of other law firm lawyers is not effective for client generation. Seek opportunities to speak to in-house counsel or industry groups so you are talking directly to potential clients and decision makers.

Most lawyers write as part of their practice, so it is natural that writing may be a good way to promote your personal brand. Law review and scholarly articles are not the most effective ways to reach potential clients. The most effective writing to attract potential clients is articles for industry trade associations or in-house counsel groups. Whitepapers and blog posts with practical information and ideas related to your target market are also good choices.

Some lawyers find that an online presence helps attract clients. If your firm doesn't prohibit it, set up a personal blog. Explore using LinkedIn, Facebook, or Twitter to promote your brand.

I've been waiting for the "Yeah, buts". Let them fly. "I don't have the time." "I don't have the energy." Well then, you don't want to be a Big Law equity partner. You make the time and energy for priorities. Activities devoted to attracting clients are priorities.

You likely did not appreciate the importance of developing clients before you started practicing law. But, there is no way around it. If you refuse to engage in client development, do yourself and your family a favor, and explore career options where developing client relationships is not crucial to professional success. There is nothing wrong with this, but you need a different career path rather than continuing the folly of pursuing equity partnership.

If you are not willing to take action to develop your client base, you will not become a Big Law equity partner. If you want to stay in the Big Law firm world, you may be a service lawyer with much lower status and compensation than equity partners. Again, that's fine if you are prepared to accept it. You will not have much security because there will always be other lawyers coming through the pipeline who can do most, if not all, that you do. And, they will do it for less money. Contract lawyers and outsourcing are also a threat to your job.

But, if you want to become a Big Law equity partner and are prepared to do the work to build your client base, you can do it. It takes a lot of work. Work that most lawyers will not do.

If you accept that you must be great at client development and take action to find clients, you will increase your chances of grabbing the brass ring, Big Law equity partnership.

LEAVING BIG LAW

You are one of the "lucky" lawyers. You scored a Big Law associate job with the big salary. Your less fortunate friends are envious. But, you're miserable. You hate your work. You're stressed or even depressed. And, you foresee no Big Law equity partnership in your future.

However, you continue working the long hours with all the stress and drudgery involved, despite it sucking out the rest of your soul. You don't believe there is an alternative. There is law school debt to pay back. You need the money to support your new lifestyle and to buy toys to provide a little relief from your life in Big Law.

Wait a minute! Is it accurate to say that there's not an alternative? Why? Because you need the Big Law salary to pay back the law school debt and support your current lifestyle? Maybe in the short-term, but is there an alternative after your law school debt is paid down?

Nope, not a chance. Not if you continue to analyze your situation in the same way. By the time your law school debt is paid down, there will be other obligations. Mortgage payments, private school tuition for the kids, and expensive vacations to get away from it all (except, you will never get away from it all).

You might be lucky enough to hang on as a salaried non-equity partner or of-counsel. Fantastic – continue to work in a job and environment you detest and discover you've hit the top of the salary charts. Also, you are much more in peril of being "downsized" when the economy, your practice group, or the firm's economics change.

Okay, let's fantasize for a minute. What if you hit the winning numbers in the lottery and became a Big Law equity partner? Your life would not get better. If you're unhappy in Big Law now, you'd still be miserable. Even more so. While you might make more money, you will be under even more stress, and with even less time to call your own while continuing to do the work you hate.

You have admitted to yourself that becoming an equity partner in your current Big Law firm is not in the cards. You may even conclude that you do not want to be an equity partner at a Big Law firm. You might even decide you do not want to practice law in any setting. Your career path (and possibly your life) seems bleak.

You're not alone. For years, the low probability of attaining a Big Law equity partnership has been well known. But, you thought you would be the exception. For your entire life, you have been an exceptionally bright and top-performing all-star, willing to do whatever's necessary to make it to the top. What went wrong?

Nothing is wrong with you. Remember that. Repeat after me, "Nothing is wrong with me. I am still an exceptionally bright, top-performing all-star willing to do whatever is necessary to be successful." Take a few deep breaths and relax a little.

After reviewing the cause of your current predicament, I will suggest how to revitalize your career and achieve success, prosperity, and personal fulfillment.

WHAT CAUSED YOUR CAREER PLIGHT?

A combination of personal and economic factors converged to squeeze the life out of your Big Law career.

Personal Factors

You may be one of the many people who went to law school by default. You never dreamed of being a lawyer while growing up, but going to law school seemed like the right decision. A passion for practicing law never grew, but your law school debt did. Big Law, at least for a few years, was the solution.

Big Law looked like the expressway to big cases, big deals, or significant social change. Unfortunately, after going through the Big Law meat-grinder, your passion was crushed.

Economic Factors

Big Law enjoyed a long run of unimagined economic prosperity for its lawyers that continued until the financial collapse of 2008. Since then, the continuing corporate push to reduce outside legal expenditures, the expansion of corporate law departments, and the growing use of technology in the legal industry have forever altered the world of Big Law lawyers.

Today, Big Law equity partners are fighting to protect and expand their personal partnership distributions. One of the easiest ways to maximize equity partner distributions is to restrict, and even reduce, the number of equity partners. What were once long odds of making equity partner in Big Law are now prohibitive. Unless you control a big book of business, you will never become a Big Law equity partner.

But all is not lost. Now is a great time to be a Big Law lawyer with a few years of experience. If you take personal responsibility for your career and do the work required to succeed and prosper.

HOW TO REVITALIZE YOUR CAREER AND LIFE

To transition out of Big Law, craft a plan to find the perfect job and create your ideal career. You must take these steps:

Recognize Your Current Life And Career

Begin by being honest about your current life and career. Assess your health, relationships, and finances. Examine your career from different perspectives. It is critical to look at your strengths and interests, and to recognize those that will be the foundation for your career going forward.

Reconsider Your Prior Life And Career

Remember your dreams and aspirations as a kid. Pinpoint the things you did that turned you on and allowed you to get into the flow. List your passions. The key here is to put aside any judgment or self-censorship, and just brainstorm ideas, activities, issues, causes, and people you were or are passionate about.

Re-Vision Your Future Life And Career

This step is fun. Look into your crystal ball and see your ideal life and career at various points. Again, no judgment or self-censorship at this stage of the process. Only dreaming.

Re-Purpose Your Life And Career

This step is where you take information from the prior steps and craft a plan of action to find the perfect job, and create your ideal career and life. The process includes deciding on your priorities, formulating a strategic plan and setting goals.

Building accountability into the process is crucial.

Rejuvenate Your Life And Career

In this step, you take actions that will help you in re-purposing your life and career. The focus is on fitness, nutrition, sleep, stress management, community involvement, recreation, and plain old fun.

Review Your Career And Life Continually

The major pieces of the process are in place, and you are implementing them. In this step, you analyze what is working and what is not. You continually refine or revise your plans and goals.

Got it? Simple, but not easy.

MOVING IN-HOUSE

The first alternative for many lawyers who've decided that practicing law in a firm is not the way for them to find success, prosperity, and personal fulfillment is to move in-house.

In-house positions differ greatly, from small start-ups or local businesses to Fortune 100 companies. The work environment ranges from traditional 9 to 5 jobs to work schedules every bit as frenetic and long as that of the most harried law firm lawyer.

The work of an in-house lawyer can also vary widely. From lawyers focused on specific tasks like analyzing the transfer tax implications of individual cross-border transactions, to general counsel responsible for all legal matters from transactions to litigation. General counsel may even handle non-legal matters.

It is easier to find an in-house position after you have a few years' experience practicing in a law firm. Businesses prefer their legal staff to be trained before hiring them for in-house positions. A lawyer's prior training and experience will dictate the in-house positions they will find most easily. Litigators will not find many positions in businesses with little litigation, and transactional lawyers will not be in demand unless the company has a substantial volume of transactions. If you are a lawyer who has specialized in FDA matters, potential in-house opportunities are limited to those companies regulated by the FDA. As a restructuring lawyer, my in-house opportunities were limited since most businesses don't need bankruptcy or workout lawyers on a long-term basis. However, I worked in-house for a few years with a company whose business focused on buying and selling distressed loans.

There is tension between specialization and general practice which is felt in the corporate world. Many businesses need lawyers with very specialized knowledge and experience. Knowledge of specific tax and regulatory issues, particular kinds of transactions, or certain types of litigation may be crucial for some businesses. For other businesses, they need lawyers with the broad knowledge and experience to analyze and advise on a wide variety of legal issues faced by the company. The more senior the position in the legal department, the broader the knowledge and experience required.

In-house lawyers are expected to be knowledgeable about the industry or industries where the company operates. You will deal with people in the business units much more frequently, and in more depth than outside counsel. You will often be part of the internal business team.

A key responsibility of in-house counsel is being the conduit between the business people and the outside counsel. You need to know the business objectives of the company and the terminology used in the industry, and be able to communicate business objectives and goals to outside counsel. You also need to know the legal practice areas and terminology in order to evaluate the performance of outside counsel and communicate the needs of outside counsel to the business people. You will be asked to explain the risks involved in particular legal strategies.

It is imperative for a lawyer to realize their purpose, passions, strengths, and interests, and have a vision of their ideal career path before they consider whether an in-house position will be the next step on their career path. A lawyer with little interest in business or in working as part of a team to achieve business goals will not be happy or successful in most in-house positions.

A lawyer focused on how law fits into the bigger picture of business objectives and strategy will be happier and more successful in-house than in a law firm.

Knowing your priorities is also critical before considering an in-house position. It is not enough to realize you are unhappy and unfulfilled in your current position. You need to examine why, and what you can change to follow a career path to more success, prosperity, and personal fulfillment. Are you suffering from the long hours required in your current position? Consideration of in-house opportunities may be an alternative, although many in-house positions now demand Big Law hours. Do you desire to be more involved in the decisions and strategy around your legal work? In-house positions provide more opportunities to interact with the decision makers and influence the decisions.

Compensation also must be considered. Traditionally, in-house jobs have not paid as much as law firms for similar work. The trade-off was thought to be fewer hours and no pressure to generate business. Today, the fewer hours' part of the equation is not as stable. While there is no pressure to produce business in the rainmaker sense, there is still a need to generate business internally for your services. In-house counsel still earns less than their contemporaries in law firms. But, senior level in-house counsel have opportunities for significant bonuses and profit-sharing arrangements.

Lawyers practicing in law firms have more freedom to set their schedules on a daily basis. Many of you will say, "What freedom? I've got partners making demands and clients calling to disrupt my schedule." Well, whatever freedom you have to set your schedule, it is much harder to do the same when your client is just a few offices away. They can drop by at any time to discuss their matter or request a quick review of something that has just come up.

HOW DO YOU LOCATE POTENTIAL IN-HOUSE OPPORTUNITIES?

First, know yourself. By now, you should recognize your purpose, passions, strengths, interests, and vision of your ideal career. If you believe that your next perfect job on your ideal career path will be an in-house position, refine your analysis and research to focus on in-house opportunities.

What strengths will appeal to businesses? Knowledge and experience in the businesses' industry and with the problems they confront are the most valuable assets. What industries have you served in your prior positions? What problems have you solved in the past?

Do you have a passion or interest in any of the industries where you have knowledge and experience? How about passion or interest for solving the problems these industries confront? Even if you have skills you excel at, and the experience to solve particular industry problems, if you have no passion or interest in the industry, you will not be happy. While you may satisfy some of your priorities, unless you have passion or interest in what you will be doing, you will not find success, prosperity, or personal fulfillment on a long-term basis.

Also, keep the vision of your ideal career in sight. How would a particular in-house position fit into your ultimate vision? Would an in-house job provide a logical way to build strengths, experience, or connections that will be useful as you move forward in your career? What are your specific objectives and goals in moving in-house?

Staying strategic in building your career path is the best way to maximize your chance of creating your ideal career. Consider the business, the industry, and the work you will do, to determine if a particular job will move you forward on your career path. Will you work on problems or with people that interest you and can help you later in your career?

Some lawyers may take an in-house position as a step on their career path without a long-term vision of staying in that position. They may want to gain more insight and knowledge into a particular industry or work on a particular issue. They may want to get more exposure to the business world and how companies operate. Or, they may want to use the position as a platform to network and build their list of contacts.

One reason you may go in-house is to create a pool of potential clients for a later move back into private practice, either as a solo/small practitioner or with Big Law. Building a book of business, or even developing a potential book of business, can be difficult while moving up the ladder at a law firm. However, to be an equity partner, you will need a substantial book of business. If being an equity partner is your vision of an ideal career, a sojourn in an in-house counsel position may not be as strange as it seems.

In-house counsel work with other in-house counsel and business people, both inside and outside of the company. The position provides a great platform to meet people who could be potential clients. It also gives you time to build a personal bond with these individuals, and to develop their trust. Unless potential clients know, like, and trust you, they will not become paying clients.

Having the experience as in-house counsel also gives you the opportunity to develop a perspective on how business approaches legal problems. As strange as it may be to some lawyers, particularly lawyers in earlier stages of their careers, the business objective is not to win at all costs. Learning to sense and understand subtler and even unspoken objectives and goals matters in achieving success. Being on the inside can help you refine this skill.

Some lawyers may use in-house positions as a way to transition their career from being a lawyer to becoming a business person or entrepreneur. While the leap from law to business will still be an issue, lawyers with experience working within a company have a narrower chasm to cross. Opportunities may appear inside the organization. And, you will be closer to the business people in the industry so you may learn of opportunities outside of the company you would not learn about if you were in a law firm.

Lawyers who envision their future career in government may also use an in-house position as an intermediate step to a job in government. Most government agencies interface or regulate specific industries or specific types of activity. You will be viewed much more favorably for employment if you worked in these industries or were involved in these activities prior to moving into government. You may also get the chance to meet and build a relationship with government employees in your work as an in-house counsel.

How do you find an in-house position? Do more research on the industries where you are interested in working. Research the best companies in that industry. Refine your research based on which companies seem best suited to allow you to satisfy your priorities. Narrow your list to 12 to 15 companies where you would like to be an in-house counsel.

Then, search your network of contacts for anyone who might have information about people in your target companies. Be thorough and creative in uncovering information and people who may be helpful. Use personal contacts and business contacts. Your personal trainer may also train the general counsel of a company on your list. Your mother-in-law's best friend may be a friend of the CEO of one of your target companies.

You can also search for job openings at your target companies. Don't spend too much time on this activity. Most of the job opportunities you will be interested in are unadvertised. But job openings, not just for in-house counsel, may give you more information on what is happening at the company, and where its current needs and issues are focused.

FROM IN-HOUSE TO EQUITY PARTNER

Your goal as a lawyer is to become a Big Law equity partner.

But, you didn't make the cut to become a first year Big Law associate out of law school.

Or, you've been a Big Law associate for a few years and don't like your chances of moving all the way up the ladder.

First, be clear you want to be a Big Law equity partner. Do you appreciate the responsibilities and obligations a Big Law partner takes on when becoming an equity partner? They are substantial, and are increasing.

Do not be seduced by the Am Law Profit Per Partner statistics. Even if accurate, they are averages. There can be a ratio of ten times or more between the highest and lowest distributions to equity partners. And don't forget, equity partnership is no longer a tenured position. More equity partners are being de-equitized every year.

What is the biggest responsibility and obligation of a Big Law equity partner? Bingo, you win. Bringing clients and revenue from client engagements into the firm. You need clients to become a Big Law equity partner, and you must continue to bring in clients to remain an equity partner. Your book of business is also the primary determinant in the equity distributions you receive. And, it is a book that starts out blank every year.

Also consider the Big Law equity partner lifestyle. It gets no easier – just different. You might control your schedule a little more, but you are still at the beck and call of your clients, your lifeblood. Your hours worked don't decline, and they might even increase. You are just doing different work – client development and relations, firm administration and management, and higher level case management. You will practice law less.

Now What?

Didn't scare you away? Those Big Law equity partnership dreams are still dancing in your head.

What can you do now to increase the chances of becoming a Big Law equity partner?

Go in-house with all due haste.

Some of you are thinking, "Yates, you seemed sane, but really?" Yes, really. Traditionally, once you left Big Law, you never went back. It was a one-way street. But, that doesn't hold true anymore. The two-way street was always common in practices that revolve around government, like regulatory and white collar work. However, it has become much more frequent in recent years in all areas of the law. The primary requirement is delivering clients immediately, or at least having the strong probability of bringing in new clients in a short time.

If you consider going in-house, what kind of position will you search for, and in what type of company, in what industry? It all depends on your purpose and passion, and on your ultimate goals. Remember, in this scenario, the in-house job is to position you for becoming a Big Law equity partner (and enjoying it when you do).

NEW LAW

You want to continue to be involved with the law. But not with any of the traditional platforms, or maybe not even as a practicing lawyer.

You've heard the term New Law, but are not sure what it is. Me either. For this discussion, we will use the term New Law to denote any employer or business that is not a traditional law firm or corporate legal department, but which provides legal services, services that support lawyers, or complementary services relating to the law.

I will not weigh in on whether some of these businesses are engaged in the unauthorized practice of law. The court decisions seem to be going in New Law's favor. There is no stopping the innovation and disruption in the legal industry, however you classify what these businesses do. Formal regulation of the legal profession will remain. But, soon the only time you will need a law degree and bar admission to do what lawyers traditionally do will be to appear before a court.

Many lawyers will gravitate toward working for New Law employers or forming their own New Law business. Lawyers not dissatisfied with the law itself, but more with the way it has been practiced and delivered. Lawyers who couldn't find their perfect jobs within the traditional framework of the legal industry will find abundant opportunities.

The New Law jobs will be more like a regular business in terms of advancement opportunities. Lawyers who want to provide legal services without some of the pressures of Big Law will find a place. Other lawyers who are more inclined to management or leadership positions will gravitate away from the day-to-day practice, and into managing and growing the business. While a third set of entrepreneurial lawyers will form and build their own New Law businesses.

These New Law employers and businesses will provide more opportunities for lawyers to align their perfect jobs and ideal careers within the legal industry. The narrow confines of what it means to be a lawyer will expand. Opportunities in different areas requiring different skill sets and interests will open. Various compensation alternatives will become available.

Whether out of necessity or out of desire, many lawyers will find their way to New Law within the next decade.

LEAVING THE LAW

Whether you are still in law school or are a senior equity partner in Big Law, you've decided once and for all that your ideal career path does not include practicing law any longer. Not in a law firm, not as an in-house counsel, not as a lawyer in the government, and not in New Law.

You have decided that something besides law is your next ideal job. Whatever your "Why," the decision has been made. But What? Where? When? How?

What will you do next? If you've worked your way through this book, you either know the answer to this question or you have a good idea of the answer. You uncovered your purpose, passions, and interests. You assessed your strengths. You envisioned the perfect job and ideal career. If you haven't done the work and don't know what to do next, go back and work through the exercises now. Otherwise, you are likely to land in a job that is not the perfect job, and not on your ideal career path. Running from an unpleasant employment situation to the next bright shiny job offered is not how to achieve success, prosperity, and personal fulfillment.

Once you decide what you will do next, the people you will serve, and the services you will offer, you will need to decide where you will do it. There are two aspects to the question of where. First, are you going to provide your services to an employer, or directly to your clients? The perceived security and infrastructure provided by an employer, or the independence and freedom of going it alone? To some extent, this will depend on your target market and the services you will offer. Even services that traditionally required a big organization with complementary services also being offered under the same roof can now be disaggregated and provided separately.

Second, where will you be when you provide the services? Will you change geographic locations, to a new city, state, or country? And, will you work out of an office, either your own or your employer's, or remotely from home, or even the beach or mountains? One reason lawyers leave the law is for the freedom to travel or work from home (or Starbucks). Other lawyers still want the benefits of having an office. You know your priorities. But, look at the benefits of different options regarding where you will be when you do your work.

When will you make the move to leave the law? Jumping too early can be just as bad as waiting too long. If you leave the law precipitously, you may give up the opportunity to expand your skills. You may also forfeit experiences or financial resources that could be useful later in a more deliberate career transition.

Lawyers who wait until their breaking point, or until they are forced to leave the law because of a layoff, health issue, or relationship issue make their career transition much harder than it needs to be. The moral is that, if you have any inclination to leave the law or make any other career change, begin well before you want to move. Most lawyers now have at least six or seven jobs during their careers. You need to be in a continual state of readiness to make your next move, and even the one after that. Like great chess players, lawyers with the most successful, prosperous, and personally fulfilling careers consider many strategies and plan ahead.

Professional Prosperity For Lawyers

All other things being equal, it is best to transition from your legal job into a non-legal job without a break. Even if you leave your last legal position voluntarily, there will always be concerns that your career transition is not a choice you made, but that it resulted from you losing your legal position because of poor performance.

How will you make the transition and leave the law? You do it the same way you would when transitioning into another legal job. You know your purpose, passions, interests, strengths, and envisioned ideal career. You know the target market you want to serve and the services you want to offer. You do your research on potential employers or clients. You filter your list of possibilities based on your priorities, and you start your job search or business start-up.

It is wise to do this well before you want or need to move. Go through the process laid out in this book. Brainstorm and network in focused areas. Bolster any skills you will use. Find experience. Meet the right people. These are all intentional efforts. If you are considering going into business by providing services relating to the discovery process, volunteer to work on a discovery matter instead of jockeying for depositions. While you may not like the nuts and bolts of discovery (who does?), you might have a passion to build a business that provides discovery services. The more you know about the nuts and bolts, the better positioned you will be to build the business.

Meet people who may be helpful when you leave the law. Do pro bono work in related areas. Volunteer in organizations related to the work you want to do. Lawyers are desired as board members, take advantage that fact.

You need to prepare for the opportunity to leave the law when it appears. Some lawyers have missed excellent opportunities for perfect jobs because they did not prepare themselves in advance. They could not take advantage of the possibilities because they were not intentional in developing their strengths, getting the right experience, or meeting the right people.

One of the most important aspects of leaving the law is presenting yourself to an employer or directly to a client as the perfect person to provide the service that will solve problems. There will always be resistance to hiring a lawyer to provide a non-legal service. There will always be others with much more experience and developed skills in the field. A powerful strategy is to genuinely portray yourself as the answer to someone's problems by providing a new perspective. That is a key to overcoming this resistance. Prepare today.

Don't burn any bridges when leaving the law, or in any other transition. As much as you may dislike the job you were doing, or even dislike people you were working with, time has the habit of changing perspectives. Some people you are working with today in the law may be people who will be helpful in your non-legal career. And, you never know – you may return to the law someday.

APPENDIX II:
LEGAL JOB SEARCH SITES

Let me briefly describe how spending time on search sites should fit into your career transition process.

First, you need to reconsider your life and career in order to identify your true purpose and passions. If you don't bring your purpose and passions into better alignment with your job and career, you will soon find the same frustrations and unhappiness in any job.

Second, recognize your interests and strengths. Not only your interests and strengths in law, but also non-legal interests and skills which you have developed in your life. Your strengths also include the unique characteristics reflected in your personality. Prepare to build on your interests and strengths in finding a new job.

Third, spend the time to envision a picture of your perfect career and life. Until you are clear about your vision, you won't know how your next job will help you move along a career path to achieve your ideal career and life.

You won't be ready to set goals and take action to revitalize your career until you've gone through the preceding steps.

You might spend a limited amount of time on legal or other job search sites. You probably will not find a job just by applying for positions on job search sites. However, you might find valuable information and leads to use in your career transition process.

There is little reason for lawyers to spend time on job search sites until they have gone through the process of identifying their purpose and passions, assessing the skills they excel at and their interests, and envisioning what their ideal career and life would look like.

Once a lawyer has done the work in the career transition process, I recommend that they spend less than 10% of their job search time on job search sites. A much more effective and efficient use of your job search time to be network, make direct contacts, and promote your personal brand.

Job search sites may be useful for uncovering terms that firms, companies, and recruiters use in describing your ideal job, though. The sites may also be helpful in identifying firms and companies in a hiring mode. Beyond that, waste little of your time on these sites.

If you have done the preliminary work, your job search efforts should be focused on making contacts and learning more about the firms, companies, and the industry where you will find your ideal job.

RECOMMENDATIONS

If you use job search sites in your job hunting process, I suggest you use these sites:

LinkedIn (https://www.linkedin.com) - The best place to locate lawyer jobs. The site also has information about employers, recruiters, and members of your professional network that will be useful in your job search.

SimplyHired (http://www.simplyhired.com) - The best of the general job search sites for lawyers at the current time.

Indeed (http://www.indeed.com) - Indeed has slipped behind SimplyHired for lawyer job searches. Both are good. You can experiment to see which one is best for your needs.

Association of Corporate Counsel Job Line (http://jobline.acc.com/jobs) - For in-house lawyer job searches.

PSJD (http://www.psjd.org) - For non-profit, government, and other public interest job searches.

I have listed none of the general career job sites that cater exclusively to lawyers. I believe they have outlived their usefulness and do not provide the value provided by the listings and search functions available in the sites listed above.

APPENDIX III:
OTHER RESOURCES

The resources in this section change rapidly and are subject to regular revision. To keep the resources and references current, I have put them on my website at gregyatesconsulting. com/ resources. The site will be updated, supplemented, and enriched regularly.

You can find PDF and Word versions of a workbook containing the questions exercises in this book, along with additional material, for download at gregyatesconsulting.com/professional-prosperity-for-lawyers.

AUTHOR BIO

Greg Yates is a public speaker, author, adviser, consultant, and coach working with highly motivated lawyers. He assists these lawyers in revitalizing their careers to find their perfect job and ideal career. His work ranges from minor career tweaks and adjustments to major career transitions.

Previously, Greg was an equity partner at two of the largest law firms in the country. He opened the New York office for one of those firms.

In his legal career, Greg built a practice of over $3.5 million a year. He represented several of the largest international banks and a diverse variety of other clients. His practice centered on corporate restructurings, turnarounds, and workouts.

In 2011, the Turnaround Management Association presented Greg with its annual award for the Large Company Turnaround of the Year.

Earlier in his legal career, Greg was in-house counsel for a publicly traded investment company, a lawyer at a boutique law firm representing the legendary New York real estate investor Harry Helmsley, and a law clerk for two federal judges.

Greg also worked in non-legal management positions at a Fortune 100 company and in several small businesses.

Greg has four graduate degrees.

www.ingramcontent.com/pod-product-compliance
Lightning Source LLC
Chambersburg PA
CBHW060008210326
41520CB00009B/855